R^{oom} in the Inn

Room
in the
Inn

Charles F. Strobel

Abingdon Press
Nashville

ROOM IN THE INN

Library of Congress Cataloging-in-Publication Data

Strobel, Charles F., 1943-
    Room in the Inn / Charles F. Strobel.
      p. cm.
    ISBN 0-687-36588-0 (alkaline paper)
    1. Church work with the homeless.   I. Title
BV4456.S77   1992
259'.08'6942—dc20

                                      92-23941
                                          CIP

MANUFACTURED IN THE UNITED STATES OF AMERICA

ACKNOWLEDGMENTS

The following pages are full of words that didn't want to be written. It's not because my editor at Abingdon Press was not encouraging. There was something within me that fought against writing them.

My editor gave me a way out. She said this wouldn't be a book as much as it would be a manual on how to set up and operate a shelter for the homeless. That seemed simple enough. In the spirit of Jack Webb, I could present "just the facts."

But that had already been done. The best guide of this kind I have found is *Working with Homeless People: A Guide for Staff and Volunteers,* published by Columbia University Community Services, 1987. It thoroughly covers all the facts about operating shelters. A copy is given to all of our participating congregations.

I saw no way to improve on that.

Then I realized that just the facts are not enough to start shelters for the homeless. Why? Because, even though the facts are out there, few people are moved by them to create shelters.

There has to be something else. What was that? I wondered.

If only I could put my finger on that particular pulse, I wold have a starting point and a direction.

As I often do, I turned to my family for help. My brother-in-law, Tom, was his usual candid self in helping me zero in on my objective. One night, while we were discussing the philosopher Joseph Campbell, Tom remarked, "It doesn't sound like he's trying to sell anything; he's just presenting a point of view for us to consider."

Acknowledgments

It struck a nerve. I quickly reacted, "That's the problem I have writing about Room in the Inn. I feel as though I'm trying to sell something, and I don't like that."

Tom countered, "Well, do you think you ought to sell it?"

"Maybe," I said; "but I wonder."

This final thought was the struggle for the following pages. It was the struggle of presenting a point of view without a hard sell. The point of view is this: sheltering the homeless is part of most religious communities' biblical heritage. The sales pitch: it's simpler, less expensive, and more rewarding than one would expect. The struggle: how do I present a point of view that I believe to be almost self-evident in a way that convinces the reader that sheltering the homeless is an *invitation,* not an obligation? Or, in Christian terms, Gospel, not Law?

As difficult as it was to write this manual, completing it was made easier by the love and support of so many people who listened, advised, and laughed me out of my seriousness about writing a masterpiece. Especially do I appreciate those who contributed with written words about their experiences with the homeless. Three people—Deby Samuels, who supplied many of the details, my cousin Pat, and my neice Beth—deserve recognition.

Most of all, I am grateful to those who are homeless, for they have given me more than I have given them in return.

To a certain extent, mine is a selfish endeavor. I won't explain that, but those who shelter the homeless know what I mean. Perhaps this manual will explain it also.

CONTENTS

FOREWORD

"What is the reign of God like? And to what shall I compare it? It is like a grain of mustard seed which a man took and sowed in his garden; and it grew and became a tree, and the birds of the air made nests in its branches."

—Jesus

Occasionally one beholds the embodiment of God's reign. The story of Room in the Inn strikes me this way: growth from a small seed into a large tree; branches for safety and rest; the amazing diversity and beauty of the people who come.

You will be moved by the story that unfolds. Just imagine, 120 congregations, from the whole range of Christian and Jewish traditions, who, once each week, transform their house of worship into an "inn" for homeless persons. Jeremiah's call to the people of God to "bring the homeless poor into your house" has been heard!

But be prepared. You too are invited to become a part of the story. Homelessness continues to grow in our nation. We have insufficient affordable housing, or livable wages to pay for housing. We have insufficient resources to help those with mental illness or inadequate education who walk the streets of our cities and towns. There is an invitation in this story.

And there is more. You will find wisdom here, an amazing range of wisdom: dealing with diversity, providing hospitality, developing an inn at your place of worship. You will find help with policies, rules, insurance, guidelines for volunteers, dealing with health issues.

So sit down and read through this remarkable story, as told by Charles Strobel. Call a friend to discuss it. Perhaps, just perhaps, you will find yourself and your congregation sharing in the next chapter by providing a room in your inn.

Read. Enjoy. And rejoice. Here is spiritual worship indeed.

—Donald F. Beisswenger
Vanderbilt Divinity School

A FOREWARNING

This manual is about something called Room in the Inn. It began in Nashville, Tennessee, in 1986.

Throughout the following pages, you will explore the possibility of creating something like it to aid the homeless in your own community.

As a beginning, it may be helpful to discuss what Room in the Inn is not and what it is.

Room in the Inn is not an attempt to resolve all of the issues of the homeless. The problems are too deep and too personal.

Room in the Inn is not a program through which a congregation takes one or more homeless people "underwing," providing them with economic assistance, job training, and personal spiritual direction.

Room in the Inn is not about establishing another large shelter downtown where hundreds of people are cared for nightly.

And it is not about boards of directors and major fundraising campaigns for capital projects.

What is it?

Room in the Inn is a way for more people in every sector to understand the problems of the homeless by becoming *directly* involved with people who are homeless.

Room in the Inn is a means through which congregations of every faith open their facilities to welcome twelve to fifteen homeless people as guests on cold winter nights.

Room in the Inn is about changing people, guests and hosts alike. It creates the environment with the opportunity for the

11

guests to learn that there are people who care . . . and for the hosts to come to understand that the faceless figure on the street corner is more than a statistic . . . and that there are solutions.

Room in the Inn is about serving without prejudice or pride. It is about accepting everyone.

Room in the Inn is about people of religion putting the tenets of their faith into practice.

Room in the Inn is not about giving; it is about receiving. It is about everyone, both guests and hosts, receiving a blessing—an encounter with God in the midst of suffering, hardship, pain, and grief.

Room in the Inn is an opportunity, not an answer. It is an experience, not a solution. In short, Room in the Inn is an opportunity to experience the presence of God in a different way.

A warning to those who are interested in reading further:

You will learn all the details you need to know to create a shelter in your church or synagogue. In fact, you may learn so much information that it scares you off. Although knowing these details is important, it will not be enough for you or your congregation to begin a shelter.

Something more is required. I am unable to give you that. You will have to discover it yourself.

CHECKLIST

They have no homes.

It is hard to look at them. The man on the corner with the black plastic bag of cans slung over his shoulder causes us to glance and then quickly look away.

A long and thoughtful look is uncomfortable, painful, maybe even threatening. To look at them forces us to break with all the social conventions of our day. For the homeless have lost all propriety. The homeless smell. They are dirty. They eat from garbage dumps. They sleep in rat-infested alleys. The streets become their toilet. How can we face them?

We go out of our way to avoid the homeless.

But for some of us, the homeless are unavoidable, even when we try to ignore them. We wonder what we can do when we realize we can no longer look away.

This manual may help. It describes how ordinary people in local congregations provide the homeless with a warm, safe place to stay overnight. And then something else happens. People who share space together—the same nation, city, street, and room—discover mutual trust and survive. And in our community, it has made a difference.

If you agree with any of the following statements, you may want to do what we did—create a shelter called Room in the Inn.

1. _____ He looks like my own father . . .
2. _____ My mother was an alcoholic . . .
3. _____ I'm afraid my son is living on the street . . .

4. _____ I'm just three paychecks away myself . . .
5. _____ I believe they have a basic right to housing . . .
6. _____ It's a sin to allow people to die on the streets . . .
7. _____ Not everybody chooses to be on the street . . .
8. _____ I wish the government would do more for them . . .
9. _____ My children could end up on the streets . . .
10. _____ I believe God wants me to do something for them . . .
11. _____ I've read about them, but don't know how to help . . .
12. _____ I wish the churches would do more for them . . .
13. _____ I want my children to know about them . . .
14. _____ I believe it's going to get worse . . .
15. _____ It's a national disgrace we treat people this way . . .
16. _____ We need more affordable housing for them . . .
17. _____ I want to find a way to help . . .

This manual can reduce your fear of facing the homeless. When that happens, your life will be changed forever, and, God willing, so will theirs.

Let me show you a few pictures of some people you may recognize:

There's Buddy, age fifty-two, who took early retirement as a sales rep and started his own business. He is conservative politically, a former college athlete, an active church member, happily married with three children. He doesn't understand why the homeless can't seem to better themselves; still he drives the van for his church shelter every week.

Paula, in her thirties, who is a claims officer with an insurance firm, married with three children. She comes every day to our downtown center to clean the toilets because someone has to do it. Her answer when someone argues that the homeless choose to live on the street, "I wonder what life must have been like for them to choose this?"

Morris, in his seventies, a former clothing store proprietor, partially disabled because of a stroke, who goes to Temple every morning for prayer, spends two to three days a week helping in the shower program, and sees his service as a mitzvah, a good deed done for no other reason than that it be done.

Bill, in his fifties, a former grocer, route salesman, recently disabled, married with children—one of whom is disabled, a coordinator at his church and a Friday volunteer in the shower program, whose special interest is finding the dishes and furniture to set people up in their apartments when they can afford it, and who never has refused to take on an extra night of shelter duty in an emergency.

Larry, in his forties, married with five children, worker at a tire factory. He first brought wood for the homeless at our center to burn outside in their oil drums, saw some of the men he grew up with, and now volunteers three nights a week.

Jerry and Jean, in their fifties, married with grown children. Jerry is a sales rep who after three nights as a volunteer declared, "My thinking about the homeless has changed 180 degrees." Jean, a nurse, comes twice a week to change the bandages of a homeless wino dying of cancer.

Gene, in his sixties, retired, reflective and philosophical, writes poetry in his free time, searching for answers, scrapes plates at a soup kitchen, works in the shower program, and volunteers one night a week at a shelter.

Linda, in her forties, married with grown children, who quit her job to devote all her time doing the clerical work for the shelter program.

There are others whom you may not recognize as easily. They can all be found sitting and talking at a local soup kitchen. Look around and see for yourself.

At one table there's Salvadore and some of his friends. They are Hispanic. Salvadore has been here for two years. He came from Mexico, speaks little English, cannot be hired because he has no green card. He is trapped and spends his time begging for money to buy a drink.

At another table is a family. They arrived in town last night. A father, mother and three children under six, a 1974 Buick with a leaking radiator and plastic covering the back window, no family or friends in town, no money, no diapers or baby food, no job, and little hope.

They are seated beside a woman in her sixties who spent most of her childhood and adult life in an institution for people with mental disabilities. She knows how to get around town and spends her day visiting with her friends along the way, walking everywhere. She never meets a stranger, and most people are kind to her. Still, her pocketbook has been snatched several times. She has been raped twice.

Next to her are two young men in their twenties. They look employable, clean, and still have some sparkle in their eyes. They work day labor at the minimum wage, make twenty-three dollars a day after the company takes out for their transportation and their sack lunch. There's no way for them to save enough for the first month's rent, damage deposit, and utility deposits necessary to move off the streets. They look ambitious, but unless they get a break and are hired full-time, they will look like the other two guys at the table in a few years.

These other two men are in their thirties, haggard and dirty. They also work day labor, but are enslaved by it. They work only when they need some money. Mostly they work to buy a drink. Their eyes show it: they have no sparkle, only resignation painted blood-shot red.

Sitting by himself is a man no one knows. He walks up and down the streets talking only to himself. He stays in a shelter, listens carefully to instructions, and follows all the rules. He is never any trouble, and no one dares to bother him. He is mentally ill. He served in Vietnam.

There they are. The volunteers and the homeless. Let's explore a way to bring them together.

WHAT IS ROOM IN THE INN?

Dateline Chicago: Homeless Man Freezes to Death

Dateline Boston: Sixth Victim of the Winter Found

Dateline Nashville: Two Homeless Men Burned to Death

Origins of Room in the Inn

It was the winter of 1985. I was the pastor of Holy Name Catholic Church in Nashville. As I looked out my bedroom window from the rectory beside the church, I saw a disturbing scene. People were asleep in their cars parked in the church parking lot, and the temperature that evening was dropping below freezing.

I was compelled to do something. I went down and invited everyone to spend the night in the cafeteria.

I didn't think too long about it, probably because I knew I would talk myself out of it. As pastor, I knew that the consequences of such a decision were far greater than simply giving a dozen men one night's lodging. What do you do about tomorrow night when they return? And the next night and the next night and on and on? One simple decision could be parlayed into a lifetime commitment. What would the parishioners say? Or the bishop? Or the neighbors?

For the moment, I decided that it was the only thing to do.

Like Scarlett O'Hara, I found myself saying, "I'll worry about that tomorrow."

What was on my mind at that moment was more critical. There were people freezing before my very eyes. It made a difference that they were right before me. There were others down the street, on the river banks, in the vacated buildings, or hovering over the sidewalk grates, but I could not see them. Somehow, it's different when they aren't right before us. Maybe it's easier to think they're someone else's problem. But that night these people were no one's problem but mine.

So I invited them in to spend the night. And they stayed the winter. Within a week other groups began to help. A friend from the Salvation Army arranged for cots, blankets, and some staff; a number of church groups brought in food every evening; and some of our parishioners became more involved. By the time the spring of 1986 arrived, there were enough people involved in the "shelter" to keep it running year round. A site was found, and Matthew 25 was born—now one of Nashville's more successful permanent shelters for the homeless.

Matthew 25 is a shelter program that offers job training and counseling for forty working men. As important as it is, it is limited in size. Hundreds of people were left out in the cold. So my problem remained: how to shelter those left out?

Holy Name Church is in the middle of a large pocket of homeless people. For many years they have been coming three times a week to the Loaves and Fishes community meal held in our parish center. Previously, many lingered and stayed to sleep in the parking lot. It always bothered me to see this. But winter time was worse, and another winter was rapidly approaching. What was a bad situation would become a deadly one. Once again, more people would be sleeping out in the cold. Once again, I wondered what could be done.

I thought about repeating what had been done the previous winter. Perhaps it would lead to the creation of another permanent shelter like Matthew 25.

But what if a new kind of shelter was formed? One that would be able to shelter expanding numbers of people in small groups, thus providing individual attention to those in need? Would it be possible to shelter hundreds of people without having to warehouse them in a large institution?

That first winter in 1985, we had helped a small number each night. Still, huge crowds remained out in the cold. If additional churches were to open their doors, in a collaborative effort, then the numbers sleeping outdoors would be reduced. Dozens of congregations around Nashville could help. Just as we had done at Holy Name, each could create in its own facility a small shelter for twelve to fifteen people.

By doing so, congregations would be putting into practice the words they preached. Their effort would be consistent with the Hebrew prophets' call to defend "the widow, the orphans and the stranger" and the Gospel mandate "to shelter the homeless."

It seemed like a workable idea and a simple one at that. It would be cost effective and yet would have a lasting impact on the lives of so many. I imagined what would happen if people put their minds and hearts into it. Maybe some people would be able to get off the streets and . . .

Thus began Room in the Inn.

Room in the Inn

In the beginning, December 1986, four congregations committed to shelter homeless people through March 1987. By the end of that winter, 31 congregations had joined. The following winter, 77 congregations were involved. In 1992, 125 congregations participated.

Room in the Inn is truly an interfaith effort. The congregations are Baptist, Disciples of Christ, Jewish, Roman Catholic, Episcopal, the Churches of Christ, Nazarene, Adventist, Lutheran, United Methodist, Church of God of Prophecy, Mennonite, Presbyterian, and African Methodist Episcopal, as well as some evangelical and pentecostal congregations.

Room in the Inn is now Nashville's second largest provider of overnight shelter during the winter, averaging in 1991–92 about 170 people a night.

Room in the Inn does not sleep people in one large facility. It consists of congregations working together to provide small, independent shelters, serving twelve to fifteen people *within their own facilities*. These congregations have committed to the principle of creating small shelters. These shelters have a:

- clean space
- manageable size
- controlled environment
- cost-efficient operation
- friendly atmosphere
- way to help people in need through one-to-one contact

The concept is simple. Typically, a church or synagogue will shelter twelve to fifteen people during one night each week. For example, seventy congregations evenly distributed over seven nights average ten congregations per night. If each takes twelve people, one hundred twenty persons are sheltered. As more congregations are involved, more people will be sheltered.

The congregations pick up their guests at a central downtown center in the early evening and return by 7:00 A.M. Hot meals are served and a warm, safe place to sleep is offered, as well as a place to wash and possibly some change of clothing.

Most important, the volunteers offer the gift of hospitality. Respect for each person is encouraged, and each person is welcomed and treated as a guest.

Over the last twenty years, interfaith activities and ecumenical projects have arisen everywhere, many of them serving the homeless. A typical program involves several congregations that contribute funds, rent a facility downtown, hire a director, and support a permanent shelter.

But Room in the Inn is different. When it began, there was no central fund, no paid director, and no downtown facility—only a sizable number of volunteers and dozens of houses of worship.

A conservative estimate is that now there are approximately 5,000 volunteers involved, forming an unprecedented mobilization of grassroots effort on an on-going basis by people who would not normally know how to help the homeless.

During a recent winter, Room in the Inn provided

- 23,120 bed spaces
- 154,424 volunteer hours
- 101,025 meals
- 20,626 snacks
- 228,926 miles driven

These are only numbers. They do not measure the heart of a group of people who truly want to provide hospitality and assistance to the homeless—and have found a way to do it.

Such growth seems phenomenal in such a short time. It could suggest that Room in the Inn has become another large agency. Yet nothing about Room in the Inn looks big and bureaucratic. It remains, for the local congregation, a small, intimate experience, akin to a gathering of friends or family. Since Room in the Inn began, participating congregations have learned that the homeless are not the only ones who benefit. Wonderful experiences are reported by both the hosts and the guests. Many congregations report that they have experienced an enrichment of congregational life. And, without exception, each volunteer develops a more realistic awareness of the complexity of the problems of the homeless.

Room in the Inn does not keep people from being homeless. But it does change people. It proves that people who are unfamiliar with the problems of homelessness can have an impact in helping the homeless. Opening their "inns" and receiving the homeless as guests bring the homeless and their problems face to face with professed people of faith throughout the region, not just in the inner core of the city.

Supplemental Programs

Once people become involved, they tend to want to do more. What began with no facilities and staff now offers help in supplemental ways year round. Presently, Room in the Inn has a storefront operation five days a week, offering additional assistance, including clean clothes and showers three days a week. This service enabled a doubling of the number of showers for homeless people in the Nashville area.

Crossroads is a twelve-week program offered through Room in the Inn and Focus (a Nashville interfaith organization) that helps a small group of people to face the problems of their past; develop the acceptable patterns of behavior to handle the present; and encourage the goals and dreams necessary to face their future. *Awakenings* is an educational program offering classes in GED preparation, literacy, job readiness training, recovery from addiction, and Bible sharing. *The Women's Group,* composed of homeless women, meets weekly to discuss issues that are critical for women on the streets.

Room in the Inn also was instrumental in launching *The Guest House.* This is a shelter program that provides an alternative to the city's "drunk tank," by receiving those who are publicly intoxicated.

These programs have evolved from the collective wisdom of the congregations. They are responses to the often asked question, "What else can we do as a group, besides what we do in our own place of worship?" But they are supplemental, not primary to Room in the Inn.

Summary

The heart of Room in the Inn remains in the local group of volunteers who, week after week, open their doors and warmly welcome strangers as guests. It is that single church or synagogue that continues to make Room in the Inn a success. Regardless of how many congregations participate, how much service they provide, and how large the organization appears to have grown, a small and intimate experience of sharing is the critical element. Each small shelter, in and of itself, has that unique opportunity to offer in a personal way the gift of hospitality.

I didn't envision any of this in the winter of 1985. I was only hoping that those twelve men wouldn't hurt one another or burn the building down. That never happened, but something else did.

OUR PLACE OF WORSHIP

When Room in the Inn began, four congregations agreed to open their doors to the homeless. On a rotating schedule they committed to shelter in their facilities twelve to fifteen people every night through the winter.

These numbers each evening would not be many, when compared with the huge numbers that needed shelter. But those four churches wanted to demonstrate that the simple idea of sheltering homeless people was possible.

They were determined to persevere, even if no others joined them. At least they would realize that they had made a difference. Perhaps the following year more congregations would decide to participate.

They did not have to wait too long. Once the news of their undertaking spread, other congregations gradually began to commit. The original group was prepared to explain the process and answer all questions. By the end of the first winter, thirty-one congregations were participating.

Some were reluctant to get involved. Looking back, I remember that although the idea was simple, and remains so, it was not easy to secure commitments. What seemed to be a proposition that was self-evident—the sheltering of the homeless in places of worship—wasn't so obvious to others.

Why? Because no one had ever done it, at least in our area. And it hadn't been done, I believe, because no one seemed to think it was possible. The idea of a shelter in a place of worship was unthinkable.

A Place of Worship—Only?

Think for a moment about your place of worship. Aren't the buildings already heated? And unused? Locked and secured? With adequate insurance? Unlike public buildings, wouldn't it be easier to gain the use of such buildings for the purpose of shelter?

I suggest six basic facts for your consideration.

1. In every community there is a great demand for emergency shelter for people out in the cold.
2. There are not enough shelter bed spaces to meet the demand.
3. Churches and synagogues have empty facilities all over the city that could provide shelter space.
4. There are plenty of people who want to help.
5. It doesn't cost much.
6. It can be done.

Sounds so simple, doesn't it?

It is simple. Still, you might object. Could your reaction reflect the significance that we as members of a congregation attach to our place of worship?

Let's think again about the place where we worship. This time let's think how much it means to us.

If we attend a service for any length of time, our place of worship usually claims a special spot in our hearts. A special meaning. It is difficult to explain exactly how important it becomes to us. But it does.

It's important for a number of reasons.

It's where we find so many of our friends.

Within its doors are many of the symbols of our faith—the Book, the table or altar, the pulpit, the tabernacle, the organ and choir loft, the baptistry, the stained-glass windows.

It's where we were married, where our children were baptized or received bar-mitzvah, where someone we loved was praised in death.

It may be a haven when we are distressed or a place of forgiveness in guilt. It offers a sense of belonging and a feeling of acceptance to so many of us.

Often, it is the gathering place for the special days in our lives, such as Passover, Christmas, Easter, Yom Kippur, Mother's Day, and Thanksgiving. When those days arrive, we find ourselves going to this place to meet others who cherish their importance.

In fact, within its walls are found those who think like us, look like us, act like us, perhaps even dress like us. It's the place where "we" as a group claim to be a community of faith, bound together by one common thread. It could be our belief or mission or history or tradition or region or neighborhood or vision or pastor. No matter what characteristics we share, we find our unity in this place.

As the community grows and becomes larger, this place seems to take on even more responsibility for meeting our needs. For example, if at one time it provided only pastoral direction, now it also helps us recreate in our own fitness center. It was always the place to hear God's word; yet now it offers day care for working parents. Once it was rather traditional in its design; now it is "multi-purposed" and adaptible to any program, plan, or mission.

A special aura begins to surround it, because so much meaning has come to be associated with it as the years have passed. More and more, it becomes sacred to us. We become protective of it.

In short, there are many reasons why it has such a special spot in our hearts and why our feelings run deep about it. Probably none is more important than the reason for our being together in the first place. Isn't it that special place where we find the presence of God?

That's it! That's why it's so important. We knew it all along but had trouble expressing it. It is there that we meet the Lord God Almighty. "Yes!" Better still, Amen.

In addition to these personal reasons, the community attaches more meaning to the building. It stands out among other buildings, like a billboard, as a testimony to everything that we believe God expects of our community—prayer and adoration, fidelity, regular participation at worship, wholesome family life, responsible citizenship, care and concern for others.

One may object by saying it's not the place but the people who worship there that is important. "The place itself doesn't matter." Indeed, the importance of our sanctuary is difficult to prove.

Much of its meaning is deeply personal, perhaps even subconscious. We may fail to recognize it. Still, I contend that our place of worship is a symbol that is vital to our memories and images of religion. It epitomizes our religion, commanding fidelity and respect.

Thus in some sort of subliminal way, in the name of God, we attach a value to our facility that in time gains such importance, its usage becomes restricted.

Sheltering the homeless in a place of worship fits none of our preconceived notions. It's not the way we normally utilize our sanctuaries.

Historical Roots

When did our buildings taken on such meaning? It wasn't always that way.

Look at the beginnings of the people of Israel and we find no permanent structure, only a movable tent. (Even today Jews recognize that if there is no synagogue, every home can become one.)

And when Jesus wanted to memorialize the time he spent with his friends and his impending death and burial, he borrowed an upper room.

Later as the early Christians yearned to remain united, they gathered in homes for the breaking of bread. Still later, persecuted and unprotected in a pagan culture, they reasoned that they did not need any buildings. In the face of their peril they believed that while the Jews and the pagans had their temples, they themselves were "temples of the Holy Spirit."

Skeptics may say their belief was merely a case of "sour grapes." Still the facts of history remain. There are no archaeological remains of any Christian edifice built for worship during the first three hundred years after the death of Jesus. Not until the conversion of the Roman emperor Constantine in A.D. 313 did the owning of property and the erection of church edifices occur.

Isn't there a message in this early history that needs to be reexamined? How is it that the Christian communities flourished in those first three hundred years? It certainly wasn't because they had magnificent structures. Historians have recognized this period as the flowering of the Christian faith, yet it was filled with persecution and martyrdom.

From a letter by Cyprian around A.D. 300 we read about such trials:

> The true state of affairs is this. [Emperor] Valerian has issued an edict to the Senate to the effect that bishops, presbyters and deacons shall suffer the death penalty without delay. Senators, distinguished men and members of the equestrian class, are to be deprived of their rank and property, and if, after forfeiting their wealth and privileges, they still persist in professing Christianity, they too are to be sentenced to death. Ladies of the upper classes are to be deprived of their property and exiled. In the case of members of the imperial staff, any who have either previously confessed or will now confess to being Christians will have their property confiscated and will be assigned as prisoners to the imperial estates.
>
> (Epist. 80: CSEL 3, 839-840)

Close observers of that age acknowledge that the willingness of the believers to risk everything—property and possessions, status and rank, even their own lives—for the sake of the Gospel was the spring that watered the seeds of faith among the pagans and changed the culture of the Roman Empire.

Perhaps this willingness to risk everything is what is lacking among the communities of faith today. Risking everything is frightening. It causes us to lose control. We have no say about the future. We cannot predict the outcome. Yet risk is at the heart of biblical faith.

Surely, no member of a congregation has a quarrel with all the biblical material supporting our helping the homeless. That material is indisputable, bordering on being self-evident. No biblical proof texts are needed to convince us. Yet putting those words into action is risky.

Could the protection and beautification of our place of worship be a symbol of an unwillingness to risk, not as individual believers, but as communities of faith? By limiting our activities there to programs that are "safe," do we as a congregation believe we will be secure in our faith?

We may not reject the notion of sheltering the homeless at the congregation on biblical grounds. But we seem to find cause to do so for other reasons. Let's explore some.

SERIOUS QUESTIONS

You are encouraged to ask questions and to anticipate problems. There are problems, of course, but they are not insoluble. Congregations recognize that there will be some glitches along the way. As you will see, through a process of trial and error, problems can be overcome.

You Say This Has Already Been Done?

Yes. It needs to be repeated. Room in the Inn shelters the homeless, not in a downtown facility, but in a congregation's very own space.

Now this doesn't mean sheltering the homeless in the actual sanctuary area; but it does mean using some other part of the facility, perhaps a cafeteria or meeting hall.

Think about emergencies when congregations open their doors to people in need of shelter. Occasionally, a disaster such as a flood or an apartment fire will bring the Red Cross and its food and supplies to set up a shelter in a neighborhood church. But that's only for a few days. What about a shelter that is more permanent? While there are not many examples, there is some evidence in history that suggests that the idea, though new to our age, is not original. Peter Maurin reminds us what an ancient Council taught. The September 1990 issue of *The Catholic Worker* reprinted his words written in 1933:

We read in the *Catholic Encyclopedia* that during the early ages of Christianity the hospice . . . was a shelter for the sick, the poor, the orphans, the old, the traveler, and the needy of every kind. . . . The fourteenth statute of the so-called Council of Carthage, held about 436, enjoins upon the Bishops to have hospices . . . in connection with their churches. Today we need Houses of Hospitality as much as they needed them then, if not more so. We have Parish Houses for the priests, Parish Houses for educational purposes, Parish Houses for recreational purposes, but no Parish Houses of Hospitality.

Room in the Inn is about establishing houses of hospitality in all the congregations of the community. It is an easy, economical, and compassionate way to offer a solution to people sleeping on the streets.

What Will Happen to Our Building?

You have an understandable concern about the building—the brick and mortar. The thought that part of your beautiful worship space be used for purposes other than for what it was designed, and then abused in the process, is disturbing. Yet the facts suggest otherwise.

Our experience of six years is that the guests respect the building and its possessions. Many of them grew up in a church and remember how they were taught to behave when going there. There's also an unwritten law on the street against stealing from a church. Few crimes are considered as terrible.

You can be assured that Room in the Inn stresses prudent caution regarding security. We emphasize this at our buildings, even when the homeless are not present. *When boundaries are set, areas designated as off-limits, and the rules for the evening made clear, there will not be a problem.* The other guests will help guarantee that.

Each year a few incidents of theft are reported, e.g., a volunteer's purse, a video tape, somebody's jacket. Sometimes, the volunteers will admit to being careless about security. If the guilty party can be identified, he or she is banned permanently from Room in the Inn; and the congregation has the option of pressing criminal charges. The other guests are often quite helpful in solving such a problem. Considered in the larger context, more than 22,000 shelter beds were provided in 1991 with only three reports of theft to our downtown office.

As for reports of vandalism—such as graffiti, broken windows, damaged walls or doors—there are none.

Occasionally, something is broken—perhaps a toilet seat or faucet. In some cases rough usage was involved, but in each case the church judged that it was not deliberate.

Now this does not mean that the shelter area—especially the showers and bathrooms—will not need some cleaning after the guests leave. Normal maintenance and cleaning is understandable considering that twelve people have used the facility for twelve hours.

What impresses many volunteers is the number of guests who offer to help clean up after themselves, so that the building is left clean.

It's Unrealistic, Impractical, and Sounds Like an Organizational Nightmare

You're right—at first glance, sheltering people in a place of worship does appear to be a major problem. But it is not as complicated as it seems. Otherwise, there would not be so many Nashville congregations doing it year after year. The experience of dozens of congregations large and small is proof in itself that Room in the Inn is a reasonable, practical, and effective way to organize an emergency shelter.

The feedback from those congregations is overwhelmingly positive. Often they are surprised at how simple and easy running a shelter can be.

There are many details of hospitality to attend to, but they are details that most people have faced in welcoming guests into their own homes.

Generally, what works at home for our friends will work at church for the homeless. You might find this hard to believe at first, perhaps because it sounds so simple. Yet it is true. A shelter at a congregation can be modeled after a home. What we like to provide our guests there—a clean, warm room, a fresh set of linens, a place to wash and bathe, some refreshing drink and nourishing food, and most important, personal conversation—we can provide at our own synagogue.

It takes simple know-how and the will to do it.

What Would a Shelter Look Like at My Place of Worship?

Take a moment and imagine your house of worship. Picture its size and how much room it has.

Are there any areas that would be large enough to house fifteen people? Is there a place to prepare food for that many? Do you have at least a bathroom nearby (or even a shower)? If you answer yes to these questions, your facility can become a shelter for the homeless.

Next you need to think about what your shelter will need. Once again, keep thinking in simple terms, not complicated ones.

To begin, imagine that you are homeless and on your way to a shelter. What do you need? Whatever you imagine that you would need in a shelter is what you will need to create your own shelter.

Your shelter, then, will need to provide the following:

- sufficient blankets, mattresses, and/or cots
- space for mattresses and/or cots comfortably arranged
- table and chairs for eating a meal
- a place to prepare and/or serve food
- enough food and drink for two meals, including snacks
- bathroom facilities
- sufficient heating and cooling
- proper ventilation
- approved safety exits with clear access
- adequate lighting
- designated smoking area (inside or outdoors)
- telephone service (posted emergency numbers)
- toiletry items (soap, towels, wash rags, etc.)
- a first-aid kit
- a fire extinguisher

What About Our Liability?

Insurance coverage is not a problem. It is already there.

My diocesan authorities advise me, as a pastor of a local church, that the parish is liable for anyone on the property, even those uninvited. So if some neighborhood boys are playing on the playground and are injured or someone takes a shortcut across the property uninvited and is injured, the parish is liable. Thus our church is required to carry enough liability insurance to cover anyone who comes onto the property. Such broad coverage necessarily includes the homeless.

Obviously, an insurance specialist should be consulted. My point is that a special insurance waiver for the homeless is unnecessary.

What Are the Policies and Rules of a Shelter?

The policies, rules, and procedures of a shelter will depend on how a local community organizes itself. There are some general principles that would apply anywhere, for example, no drinking, drugs, or violence.

Whatever the policies and procedures are, they need to be clear. Rules seem bureaucratic and can be cumbersome. But the lack of them inevitably leads to enormous difficulties, both with hosts and guests. Neither will know the boundaries of the program. You and other volunteers will be confused about issues of decision-making and other responsibilities. You will not be able to answer simple questions with confidence. You will feel insecure before the guests. The guests will sense your uncertainty. They will have less trust in you. This potentially could result in the guests themselves attempting to take charge or presuming a freedom to do whatever they want.

Policies and procedures also need to be fair. One of the first things we learn as children is a sense of fairness. How often have our children said, "It's not fair." Rules, then, need to be fair and applied consistently. The guests will sense when something is not fair and complain about it. Over the years at Room in the

Inn, we have found that cooperation among guests is directly proportional to the sense of fairness they feel about the rules.

When Room in the Inn began, we had only a few basic policies and procedures. But they were clear and applied to all. Now they remain our basic policies and rules, with only a few modifications.

The following policies and procedures have been adopted by the board of Room in the Inn. *We make them known to all guests at our downtown center during their interview.*

Room in the Inn is a common effort of various groups, religious congregations and organizations who, in the name of God, offer a safe place of overnight shelter to men and women who are working to get off the street, re-establish their home life, and bring stability to their lives once again. This is our basic commitment to you, our Guest.

Each Inn considers you its guest for the night, one of the family. As with any family there are some basic guidelines that must be followed. In order to be a real part of this family for the evening, you must commit yourself to observe these guidelines.

1. Each guest will be interviewed each night before being placed on a transportation list.

2. Guests will be picked up in the evening at Room in the Inn and returned to the same location about 7:00 A.M. Persons who need to be back earlier than 7:00 A.M. for work should seek a congregation on the bus line. The host is not obligated to provide early transportation to work.

3. Once a person is on the van, he or she is responsible to the host. All the guidelines apply both to the time in the van and at the congregation.

4. There is to be no drinking.

5. Weapons are not permitted.

6. Drugs are not permitted. Any and all prescription medication must be made known to the host or hostess.

7. Fighting is not permitted.

8. Foul language or verbal abuse of any one of the hosts or hostesses for the evening will not be accepted.

9. Each guest shall respect the property of other persons and of the congregation or sponsor.

---

10. Cut-off time for registration and sign-up is the same each night.

11. Provided all the guidelines are observed, tickets will be provided the following morning to each guest for the next night's lodging.

Remember that the host/hostess for the evening is in charge and will help in any way possible. So, ask questions, seek advice, and know that every volunteer is there to help. We hope your stay with us at Room in the Inn is a pleasant one.

Additional policies, rules, and procedures will be needed relative to each congregation's needs. For example, a congregation may designate a smoking area, areas that are off-limits, a routine for setting up and taking down cots, procedures for getting clothes from a clothing room, rules concerning showers, and so on. These are announced to your guests when they arrive, as part of your welcoming remarks. In announcing the rules, remember to invite the guests to observe the rules, rather than order them like a drill sergeant. You need not worry. The guests expect some order and are quite willing to cooperate. For a sample procedures guide, see Appendix, sample B.

Although particular rules and procedures are necessary, a general rule of organizing is to keep them simple and have as few as possible. See Appendix, sample C.

Finally, policies and procedures need to be evaluated and updated periodically.

FURTHER CONCERNS

It's Wednesday night. Your guests are getting settled, and someone asks you for a bandage. When you look at the injury, you notice blood and apparent swelling. What do you do?

Would you know what to do if someone started choking?

What About Emergencies?

Any condition that is life-threatening is an emergency. The Emergency Medical Team (911) should be called. In case of doubt, it is still best to call and let 911 make the decision. Some shelters have a nurse or doctor in the congregation on call to offer advice or assistance. See Appendix, sample A, for emergency medical guidelines.

Each local municipality has a policy about ambulance and medical fees. Most waive fee requirements for the indigent. Still, the issue needs to be clarified.

Guests are expected to make known all prescription medicine upon arrival. This is an appropriate time to assess the nature of one's illness and to be on alert for the evening.

Some situations are predictable, although not necessarily probable, e.g., a person withdrawing from alcohol may have seizures at any time, but especially in the twenty-four through seventy-two hours since last drinking. One guest had five alcohol withdrawal seizures in one of our churches. The paramedics were called, and he was taken to the hospital. Had he been outdoors, as he often was at night, the doctors say he probably would have died.

At Room in the Inn, our experience has been that in a month's time, averaging 170 beds a night, medical emergencies are reported about twice a month. There are, however, more frequent cases that go unreported. Generally, they are handled with supplies from a first-aid kit. It is recommended that the first-aid kit be easily accessible and completely stocked at all times.

If your congregation doesn't have a first-aid kit, or if your kit is missing a few items, here's a list of items that the American Red Cross recommends:

- [ ] Latex gloves—2 pairs
- [ ] Gauze pads—104" x 4" and five 2" x 2"
- [ ] Sterile bandaging tape—1 roll
- [ ] Adhesive bandages—assorted sizes
- [ ] Sting kill
- [ ] Sterile saline solution
- [ ] Peroxide
- [ ] Antibiotic ointment
- [ ] Betadine prep pads
- [ ] Syrup of ipecac
- [ ] Cold pack
- [ ] Tweezers
- [ ] Scissors
- [ ] Needle
- [ ] 2 paper bags
- [ ] Waterproof matches
- [ ] First-aid posters, particularly on adult CPR and adult choking
- [ ] A list of contents for restocking purposes

The items listed below will expand your first-aid kit to a medical-emergency preparedness kit.

- [ ] Thermometer
- [ ] Aspirin (300 mg.)
- [ ] Acetaminophen (such as Tylenol, 325 mg.)
- [ ] Ibuprofen (400 mg.)
- [ ] Benadryl (for itching)
- [ ] Decongestant (or other remedy for stuffy or runny nose)

☐ Alcohol-free cough syrup
☐ ABC fire extinguisher
☐ Non-electric can opener
☐ Radio with extra batteries
☐ Flashlight with extra batteries
☐ First-aid book
☐ Battery-operated clock or watch

First aid is something we gamble with every day, but when an emergency arises, our success or failure—and the health of a victim—may depend on how prepared and how up to date we are on first-aid equipment and techniques. Ideally, every host congregation should have on site someone trained in CPR and first aid.

What About Illnesses, Injuries, and Communicable Diseases?

Everyone at one time or another wonders about "catching something." There is always this possibility, but similar risks are encountered by anyone who uses public restrooms, makes hospital visits, or has any close contact with the public.

All of us have the usual medical problems that plague us from time to time, such as the common cold, coughs, and the flu. Homeless people suffer these ailments also, as well as other medical problems that result from the poor nutrition, exposure, poor hygiene, and other circumstances unique to their life-style. For instance, a watchful volunteer will recognize someone with respiratory problems, hypothermia, frostbite, and skin disorders from constantly being in the elements. The homeless also experience trauma from accidents and assaults. Their legs and feet are often swollen and ulcerated. They lack adequate dental care and eye care.

In the event that there is a problem, some medical attention may be needed at once. A general rule is to check with a qualified medical person or consult a local hospital emergency room. There also should be a system of referral for the volunteers. At Room in the Inn, volunteers are asked to refer all health matters to our office or directly to Nashville's clinic for the homeless.

The local public health department, not your congregation, is responsible for controlling the spread of contagious disease. Its staff should be included in a training session for volunteers to explain how to treat guests suspected of being contagious.

Tuberculosis (TB), Acquired Immunity Deficiency Syndrome (AIDS), hepatitis, and lice are common communicable diseases. They may exist among shelter guests. You can take preventive measures, such as using paper products and following proper handwashing procedures, to reduce the risk of infection.

Tuberculosis (TB) is a contagious disease, affecting the lungs. Its germ is airborne, but does not live long after leaving the body. Thus the likelihood of volunteers and guests contacting TB from a guest is minimal. Your public health department can provide free on-site screening of volunteers and guests, a service that relieves everyone. This should be done once during the winter months.

HIV, the virus that causes AIDS, is not highly contagious, but may be the most alarming. Everyone needs to be educated about how to prevent the spread of the disease. Once again, your local health department should be involved in education and training.

Hepatitis is a disease of the liver. There are two types, A and B. A jaundiced complexion is the best signal of an infection. Any guest who is jaundiced should have a medical evaluation as soon as possible, and a referral may be necessary. No sharing of eating or drinking utensils and proper handwashing are the best prevention.

Another problem that can occur—and that we can help prevent and bring relief from—is lice. Due to scarce opportunities to practice personal hygiene, this can be an uncomfortable problem.

Lice are either scabies or crab lice. Scabies are mites that burrow into the skin and appear as red spots usually on the wrists, elbows, fingers, or other skin fold. Crab lice, recognized by the visible white nits on their eggs, can be found in the head and other body hair.

Lice can be treated with lindane lotion and shampoo and eliminated simply by following the directions on the label. To help prevent infection or reinfection, wash in hot water any bed linens and towels used by the guests. Use a recommended spray in the rooms, bathrooms, and on mattresses. You shouldn't have any fear of catching lice from the guests. There must be contact in order to pick them up; lice can't "jump" or fly across space.

Lice infestation is not a pleasant problem, but if someone is infected, a gentle yet private conversation can ease embarrassment and offer relief. The other guests are like radar and quickly report any "sightings." Still, we have had very few incidents of it, largely owing to the increased availability of showers in the churches. The more opportunities for bathing, the less the chance for lice and other skin ailments.

What About Disorderly Conduct?

Physical and verbal abuse, as well as drugs and alcohol, are forbidden. But sometimes tempers flare when cold, hungry, discouraged people are in close proximity. And the same problems that contribute to conflicts in society at large are found in the shelter.

At Room in the Inn, a lot of tension is eliminated before the guests are transported to your facility. Our staff is familiar with those personalities that have trouble getting along, so they are not placed together at the same shelter. Having a central gathering place allows time for potential problems to surface and be resolved before they ever get to your shelter. The guests also are aware that they can ruin a good thing if they misbehave. There is a lot of peer pressure to be on one's best behavior. Overall, there are few reports of disorderly conduct. During an average week, sheltering 170 guests per night, there may be two to four incidents of disorderly conduct reported.

If a problem should arise, there are some actions that help reduce conflict.

Be sensitive to any indicators of developing tension. Treat the troubled guest as you would want to be treated. Try to resolve arguments peacefully, but know your limits.

Never put your hand on another person. On the street, this is the equivalent of throwing the first punch. Never take sides in an argument, but try to see both sides. This will win respect for you. Stay calm always, speak softly, and ask people to separate from one another. A cooling off period may be all that is needed to save face.

Don't preach, shame, or talk down to anyone. Allow for a reasonable time to resolve the matter and then ask for each side to end the dispute. Do not hesitate to call the police if the situation develops into a crisis.

At Room in the Inn, we do not know a person's criminal record. I presume that we have in our population a cross-section of every possible criminal charge. I do not mean that all homeless are criminals, but there are convicted felons among the homeless. In fact, some prey upon the others. This still does not deter us. The clear statement of policies regarding violence and the practice of hospitality establishes the boundaries that prevent serious trouble from erupting.

What About People with Mental Illness?

Some of the homeless suffer from some form of mental illness. Be sensitive to the needs of anyone who appears "different." Do not "crowd" such guests. If they want to stay apart, leave them alone. Note anyone you think needs help from a mental health clinic and make the necessary referral as soon as possible.

If there is an "episode" (some strange or abnormal behavior), stay calm and reassure the guest that he or she is safe and in no danger. Call the 911 number for the paramedics.

The mentally ill are easily singled out in a crowd, because the other guests give them plenty of space. Not knowing the nature of their illness, the others still have a healthy respect for it. Mental health professionals among the homeless agree that the mentally ill are more likely to hurt themselves than anyone else. This has been our experience at Room in the Inn.

What About Suicide?

A suicide threat is a cry for help that cannot be ignored. While the threat of suicide is sometimes manipulative, you must take any suicide threat seriously.

Tennessee law requires that our staff and volunteers notify either the police or the paramedics when a person verbalizes the intention to commit suicide. Whether or not a person actually intends to follow through on the threat, it signals profound emotional pain. In every case, further evaluation by a mental health professional is needed. By bringing the required professionals into the problem, the congregation and the volunteers pass the liability on to the proper authorities.

If someone is threatening suicide, take the following steps:

1. Remain calm.
2. Have another volunteer notify the police and/or paramedics.
3. Stay with the guest at all times until the proper authorities arrive.
4. Offer support to the guest.
5. Ask the guest to surrender any belongings that potentially are harmful—belts, shoelaces, pins, lighters, and so on. Use your imagination. Everything is a potential weapon for those serious about suicide.
6. As a rule, do not tell the person that the authorities have been called. It may create more anxiety and panic. The authorities will explain their presence once they arrive.

At Room in the Inn, our records reflect three to five cases of suicide threats per year out of fourteen hundred guests.

What About Sleeping Arrangements for Couples?

Shelters are set up to take single men, single women, couples, or combinations of all three. Dealing with both sexes is not as difficult as it may seem.

There is no general policy about sleeping arrangements. Each congregation sets its own rules. Some allow couples to sleep on cots next to each other, with rules concerning space between mattresses. Others keep the men and women separated.

Whatever a congregation decides, everyone understands that the rules of the congregation apply. Guests are never told by the downtown staff that they can be the exceptions to the congregational rules. But be aware that sometimes guests attempt to get volunteers to bend the rules about men and women sleeping together by saying that our downtown staff "said they could."

What About Families?

Of all the people on the streets, none is more vulnerable than a family. Families present a special set of circumstances. We worry about the women and children. Room in the Inn gives us a unique opportunity to care for them at least for the night.

Provide some privacy, milk and juices, baby food and diapers, children's clothes, a place to bathe, toys, books for children, and whatever else children need. A separate sleeping area is recommended, providing the family with some privacy. It also allows the other guests some quiet time so that they are not disturbed by any children crying or upset during the night. An early evening pick-up time also guarantees that the children can be fed and put to bed before the rest of the guests.

Remember that homeless parents have their children with them all the time. They never get any time for themselves apart from the children. They cannot afford to leave them in the care of another. There is no one to trust. Imagine their stress.

Volunteers are people whom they can trust to care for their children for a while. Children of volunteers can offer a lot of help playing with the children. One volunteer remarked that his own children now realize "how tough things can be; they appreciate their own home, and that cuts down on the 'I've-got-to-have-this-or-that' syndrome."

What About Transportation?

At Room in the Inn all guests are transported together in vans or cars provided by the congregation. Guests are not allowed to drive their own cars to the shelters. They leave them parked at our downtown center. Guests are reminded that the congregations are expected to bring them back downtown by a certain time. Perhaps some may make an earlier trip back for those going to work early, but guests are reminded not to expect it.

What About Money?

It is a common understanding among volunteers that giving money to any guest is not a good idea.

A Final Word

In general, your concerns are normal ones. Your training session should address them in more detail with local homeless advocates and professionals providing the leadership. Once the shelter is under way, anxieties and fears subside as the volunteers gain experience. And the consistent application of the rules and procedures of the shelter gives security to the guests.

WHAT SHOULD OUR VOLUNTEERS EXPECT?

It was an early October evening flight from Atlanta to Nashville, just after take-off, and the Boeing 737 soared upward. Rising majestically, yet ever so softly and silently, we headed toward the northwest. Those of us sitting on the left side had a magnificent view of the sunset. Already the setting sun had dropped below the horizon. Only the burnt-orange trail of the sun's glowing embers illumined the landscape—the last, lazy light of a long, dying day.

As the plane climbed higher in altitude, something strange seemed to happen. The sun—only moments before having slipped beyond the edge of our view—reappeared. Its ball of energy began very slowly to "rise" over the land, creating for us the illusion of morning.

The timing was exact. As we surged higher and higher with ever-increasing speed, we seemed for a while to be catching up with time. But it was only for a moment. Despite our chasing it at a high speed, the sun played a game of tease. It began to slip away again and once more drop below the surface of the earth.

We could not go fast enough; we couldn't keep up. The engines seemed frantic now, no longer quiet. They urged us forward, almost desperately.

Still, the sun continued to sink and slowly to disappear, a second time, never to be seen for the rest of that day.

With a tantalizing longing, I found myself leaning forward in my seat and arching my neck to look over the edge of our world for that one final, lasting glance of that day's darkening light.

I found myself wishing that we'd taken off a few minutes earlier, wishing that the plane had gone faster to keep up, wishing that I had gazed upon the first sunset more intently, wishing that I could freeze this moment in time, wishing, wishing, wishing . . .

I turned away from what I had planned to do and became intrigued with what had just occurred to my left. The passing of the second "sunset" brought on a new sensation of amazement. What a lovely feeling of wonder I noticed that I was enjoying! The glow of the sun may have vanished in the night, but I now experienced an inner glow. Call it a brief insight or more an intuition. Whatever it was, it was worth treasuring and I became lost in it.

My mind began to race with images and ideas. I was learning lessons again, like discovering pictures hidden behind unconnected dots until connecting lines are drawn between them.

Suddenly, I was making connections between unrelated and otherwise isolated or solitary incidents and experiences in life. What may have required proof at some other time was now obvious. Things—issues, problems, situations, people, relationships—that before may have seemed confusing now became clear.

Those in the drug culture probably would have called this a rush. The word is apropos. The rush of images was too much to comprehend and analyze all at once. All I could do was to allow the sensations to linger and leave whatever insights my mind could gain from them. There was no rational explanation for what I was enjoying, nor was there any time limit on it. I was lost in introspection. Time was racing by so fast that the hour trip seemed only a few minutes.

How a sunset could trigger this series of mental experiences and the subsequent fast-forwarding of time is beyond my understanding. All I know is that something I never expected to happen on that flight did happen, and I felt enriched because of it.

Experiences such as this are not uncommon. People have moments of ecstasy, of coming to awareness, of insight. Abraham Maslow writes of these moments as "peak experiences" in life.

Generally, they are unplanned, unexpected, and unrehearsed. They may occur anywhere. They are deeply personal and private. Others may share the same experience but react differently. They may listen to our explanation but must remain forever outside it. Only by remembering a similar experience in their own lives can they hope to identify with what we may have experienced.

These moments are the special times that stay with us, long after other, more mundane times are forgotten. These are seldom forgotten. They can be recalled easily, but never enjoyed as they were experienced originally.

Such moments are real, not fantasy. They are close to the center of our being, the core of our inner selves. They bring feelings of awe, wonder, surprise, amazement, and joy. We use language to describe them but often our words fail. Poets capture these feelings best. They are different from those "highs" that are conjured up artificially through the use of hallucinatory drugs and other stimulants. The "rush" from drugs distorts reality. Moments of ecstasy help us to see life as it truly is.

Everyone is able to experience such moments and has from time to time. Sometimes people experience them in giving shelter to the homeless.

Jenny, a volunteer in a large, suburban church, writes:

"How like us they are! Treated with dignity, they behave in a dignified manner; shown respect, they are respectful; treated with warmth, they thaw. They must have experienced pain and degradation as well, for the evidence is visible, sometimes rising to the surface.

". . . a veteran who walks with great difficulty, thanks to bullets that destroyed the bone in his right leg from the knee down. Subsequent surgeries substituted a steel rod, a little too short. His disability check goes mostly for alcohol; that provides anesthesia for Vietnam memories but deters healing. Neither does much for his anger.

". . . a family of four, unable to earn a living in Florida, takes the next AFDC check and sets out for Indiana, where the woman's adoptive mother has promised help. They run out of gas in Nashville, and Father Strobel asks if they can join our group for the night. There's a chance for this couple if luck holds. They're scared, but the cycle of failure and

46

hopelessness hasn't set in. One of our hosts slips out and buys stuffed animals for the anemic two- and four-year-old boys, telling them she 'ran into Santa.'

". . . a young man from the Nashville area, feeling isolated at first because he's the only black in the group. Poverty makes no class distinction, yet racism runs rampant among rich and poor alike.

"So this tired, hungry, cold, shabby group of fifteen eats the meal, takes showers, picks through clothing, and settles for the night on mattresses arranged in a temporary semblance of private space. Their gratitude is immediate but will fade by tomorrow, when it's back to square one for them, back to normalcy for us—a big dividing line that our sincerity and sympathy can't span.

"Today, I take a daytime nap (in the relative luxury of my own bed, under a roof!) and dream that my son and I are on the streets, subsisting on the kindness of strangers. When I awaken, I think back to last night. An innocent SNAFU had caused our van to be quite late picking up our guests, and they were shaky with hunger by the time they arrived. I had joined them at the table and kept apologizing until the young black man quietly stated that it was for the best, that the delay had made it possible for the family of four to join us, since they had arrived long past the regular pick-up time. He was comforting *me*. How kind he was!

"We hear from time to time how easily we could become like the homeless. Just as true: how like us they are."

What Jenny went through is one of countless experiences that volunteers report after helping in the Room in the Inn. They are that added bonus that accrues as people invest their time and energy in being of service.

No one ever plans on such experiences occurring. Mostly, the hosts for the evening have their minds and hearts set on providing a pleasant evening for each guest. Then, a twist, a reversal of roles or an unexpected display of compassion and understanding, and our preconceived ideas are brought tumbling down. Like the sunset that reappears, it's as if we are given a "double take"—another glimpse at a world of judgments and conclusions we so neatly wrapped that the light of a new insight could not enter.

This second look illustrates what may be a lesson about life itself. Often we fail to notice what is important the first time around. College students drift through classes half-heartedly, drop out, and then return later after entering the work force. Their appreciation of school and the opportunity it affords to learn increases the second time around.

Second chances are often better. Volunteers in shelter programs get a second chance. They have another opportunity to look at the homeless, other than the way they normally see them—from a distance.

This second time, they are asked to consider them as guests. Not as patients, inmates, clients, problems, or cases—but as guests. It requires a new way of thinking and acting. Instead of controlling and managing the homeless, the host who considers them guests for the evening serves them.

The Role of the Servant

This is no small or easy task. Consider those places where we expect to be served. Two appropriate examples are hotels and restaurants. What do we expect of bell hops, desk clerks, waiters, and busboys? Nothing less than perfection in serving us. We justify ourselves by saying that we are paying for such service. They are working for us. They are at our beck and call. It makes no difference that we leave them a generous tip when they treat us well. They are our servants. We expect to be served.

The hotel and restaurant industries promote this mentality. They teach their employees that the customer is always right, even if the customer really isn't. We've heard the slogans before. "Please let us know if we can be of any service." "We aim to please." "How may I help you?" "If there is anything else that you need, just call."

There are many ways a volunteer can relate to the homeless. One can be a drill sergeant, a police officer, a warden, a supervisor, an observer. None is as humbling as the role of the servant.

Why? Because of the role reversal that is required. We must

change our attitude from being superior to being of service. It isn't easy. The externals suggest otherwise.

Look at how the homeless dress ... speak ... smell ... behave. It's not the way we act. It's easy to draw conclusions that the way we dress and speak and smell is the right way.

We are taught about first impressions. They are lasting. These externals are our first impressions. They are there as we see the homeless from a distance, and they are there when they walk into our church for the first time.

To become a servant in their midst involves placing ourselves at their beck and call. Just like the clerk waiting on the customer who is always right, we aim to please.

This way of thinking seems risky. Actually, it is, but not the way that we first imagine. We assume that we will be overrun by the guests. They will take advantage of us and our kindness. We will lose control.

The truth is that we do lose control. But what takes over is not the homeless running around helter-skelter, but the power of love that we call *hospitality*.

Hospitality

What is this notion that we call hospitality? John Cogley writes of it this way:

> This is the ideal of hospitality: being sister to sister, brother to brother, children of the same parent. Not scientific social work—hospitality. No condescending judge dealing with errant accused—hospitality. No, hospitality is derived from the Latin word for "guest." It expresses a relationship between equal people: host and guest. It is bound by the rules of courtesy and human companionship and ruled by the law of charity.
>
> There are always men and women who need hospitality for one reason or another. There are in an imperfect world of imperfect men and women always those who need a calling back to life, a restoration of personality. There are always those lonely people in all times, in all places, who need the knowledge of being respected as men and women, of living with other men and women with dignity, of sharing their own burdens with others and bearing some of the burdens for others.
>
> Hospitality reminds people that they are sisters and brothers, children of God, dependent on others and capable of being depended on by others.

It is not a specialized work, requiring scientific training. It is something for everyone to practice according to the measure they are able to do.

The charm of hospitality, because it is peculiarly human, appeals to all people. . . . It is not surprising that often God should use the hospitality people give each other as an instrument of God's grace.

If the mission of the shelter is to provide a warm, safe place to eat and sleep overnight, the principal means to accomplish that mission is to provide the gift of hospitality.

Physical shelter, food, clothing, a place to wash, safety, personal comfort, and caring persons as volunteers are all a part of this gift. But the primary expression is the unconditional love and respect that we show for all who come for shelter.

We consider them our guests for the night, one of the family of God. We hope that the kindness we show them will help them get off the street, reestablish their home life, and bring stability to their lives once again.

Providing the gift of hospitality cannot be faked. We cannot truly serve and at the same time bear silent resentments. It will not be real service, but a form of trickery or manipulation. The guests will sense our reluctance and perhaps our rage.

Accepting them and seeking to serve their needs puts them on a level of equality with us. It gives them dignity and importance. They begin to believe we actually care for them as they are, not as we want to them to.

Serving the guests puts us on a level of equality with them. By seeking to serve them and to be available to them, we discover something in ourselves that they themselves are facing—humbling experiences that ignore them and take advantage of them. For as we serve, we too experience the humbling snub of being unappreciated and used.

Of course, most of the guests do appreciate our kindness. We have no problem with them. It's the way we expect them to act. It reinforces our importance.

The unappreciative are another matter altogether. How do we feel about them? Why aren't they grateful? Why should we serve them?

Gayle, a volunteer in a small, urban church writes:

"Some Sunday nights were easier and more peaceful than others, and some Sundays, I felt better equipped to handle the individual personalities and needs of our guests. I can remember a particularly stressful Sunday when I had just about given all I had to give. The well was empty.

"One of the guests that evening was a young woman, probably late teens. From the moment she entered our building, she was miserable and unhappy and she didn't care who knew it. My attempts to appease her were feeble at best and the two of us spent the remainder of the evening just trying to stay out of each other's way.

"I slept that night on the couch in the back room and I prayed before falling asleep that God would give me the patience I needed to get my guests up, fed, and on their way the next morning.

"I awoke at 5:00 A.M. and began our early morning routine. I made coffee, set out juice and doughnuts, and retrieved the lunches, prepared the night before, from the walk-in cooler. By this time, the guests were beginning to shuffle around sleepily. Some went to the bathroom, others sat at tables and smoked or began eating their meager breakfast.

"I noticed almost immediately that my annoying friend from the night before continued to sleep in a far corner. With purpose to my step, I went toward her, relishing the fact that I had the opportunity to return a small portion of the aggravation I had suffered at her hands the previous night. As I approached, I could see she was curled tightly into a fetal position, and I could hear a muffled sucking sound coming from her. Standing over the sleeping woman, I looked down and saw the little girl she must have been; warm and content in her bed, busily sucking away on her favorite thumb. There was no anger or rage or fear. There was just the child this woman had once been. The child that was still lurking inside and who sometimes made herself and her needs known in a very loud and obnoxious way.

"I watched her sleep a little longer and quietly I walked away, giving her the chance for a few more minutes of restful and healing sleep."

At times like these, we are faced with taking a second look. This time we look inwardly at the way we see our service. We face a dilemma. We either continue to serve grudgingly or we see no reason to continue . . .

Or we come to terms again with those haunting words, "If you love those who love you, what merit is there in that?"

GUïDELINES FOR VOLUNTEERS

A shelter depends totally on volunteers. They need training and coordination to become a group that works together as a team. Not everyone can or should be a shelter volunteer. To become a host or hostess, keep in mind several specific points.

Your Motivation

If you are interested in volunteering, take a moment and ask yourself, "Why?" What draws me to sign up as a host or hostess for an evening? Jot that down and remember it.

In a church-sponsored shelter, one would think that the Gospel of Jesus is the reason one serves. It may be the overarching motive. Still, there are others that are rooted in our culture, history, philosophy, personalities, and personal experiences.

There may be several reasons. The checklist at the beginning suggested some of them. Some seem better than others. They range from anger and guilt to wanting to make a difference in our world. Any and all reasons bring people to work in shelters. Why is it useful to identify them? Motives count. They reflect the way we interact with guests. For example, if guilt is my motivation, I may have trouble saying no to any request. Wanting to save the world may be the reason I want to invite some guests to move in with me.

Whatever my motives, they will be, by necessity, mingled with the motives of others. That mixture does not mean that volunteers will be in conflict. People with different motivations do not have to agree on all aspects of the problems of the homeless. They can work well together, provided all follow the procedures and stay within the limits expected of everyone.

Your Ability to Set Limits

Licensed professionals speak of establishing boundaries in any helping relationship. This is for the protection not only of the host, but also the guests. Overstepping those limits can create serious problems.

I remember a volunteer who was drawn to help some men beyond the regular night shelter. She volunteered to meet them during the day to transport them to work. Eventually, she was doing other things for them, including the purchasing of drugs.

Other examples are not so clear. The following check list will help you imagine some. They are signs of unhealthy boundaries.

- being overwhelmed by—preoccupied with—a guest
- going against personal values or rights to please others
- accepting food, gifts, touches, or hugs you don't want
- touching a person without asking
- falling in love with a guest
- letting the guests direct your life
- telling all
- acting only on impulse
- creating your rules rather than following procedures
- promising what you cannot fulfill
- giving out your telephone number or street address
- criticizing other service agencies or congregations

Generally, there is little time to develop a relationship with the guests. You have your guests for approximately twelve hours, most of them sleeping hours. Chances are, your face-to-face time with the guests is less than three hours. This simply isn't enough time to do what you would like to do—that is, help attack the central problems of a person's homelessness. A guest brings too many problems, developed over too long a period of time, for one to be able to do more than offer some kind word of support and encouragement for the evening.

This is especially difficult for people of faith. We want to fix things. Immediately. Faced with the overwhelming needs that walk into our shelter, there is all the more reason to be clear about our limits.

How to Create a Hospitable Relationship

Despite the limits of time, you can make a difference in a person's life. By offering the gift of hospitality, you offer hope and inspiration.

Several elements are involved in starting this relationship. For most volunteers, the first thing to overcome is a fear of saying or doing something wrong.

How should I approach a guest?

• Introduce yourself and let the guest know your role. "Hello, I'm John. I'll be staying overnight if you should need anything."

• Be aware that some guests may be "regulars" and know your program, but chances are, most don't. Or they get confused, understandably, with other congregations. Make sure you let everyone know the basics: any special rules, where the restrooms are, what the evening's schedule will be, what time they will be awakened, whom to contact if they have a question or need.

• Out of consideration for the guest, avoid putting him or her in a position of having to respond initially; he or she may not want to talk.

• Let the guest warm up to you at his or her own pace. If guests don't want to talk, let them have that gift of comfortable silence.

• Do not expect the guests to reveal personal information about themselves, and vice-versa.

• Avoid excessive questioning. While you may interpret that as interest, the guest may see it as prying. The closest thing to a true diamond is a clever imitation. There is a real difference between interest and curiosity, though they look alike. One is a concern for the other person; the other is a personal need. Know the difference as you engage in questioning the guest. Furthermore, they are asked personal questions constantly by social service agencies, clinics, and so on. Not having to answer those questions may bring more comfort than a well-meaning attempt to engage them in conversation by asking them.

• Always use a calm tone of voice. It is soothing and indicates confidence in your role and your acceptance of them.

• Look at the person to whom you are talking and give him or her your full attention. Try not to stand over a seated guest but meet at eye-level.

• See each guest as an individual. Avoid stereotyping them. The more guests you meet, the harder it will be to label them.

• Be honest. Be able to say, "I do not know." If you are asked, give your opinion about an issue, such as a guest's drinking habits, but in such a way that it is constructive, not judgmental. Unsolicited judgments may create arguments and resentment.

• Mingle with the guests, talking to those who are willing to talk. Try to avoid a situation where hosts are huddled together just talking with one another. This will only make your guests feel even more "different" and unacceptable. Open your conversation to anyone who wants to participate.

• Remember, you are in comfortable, familiar surroundings. Your guests are in a strange territory with strange people. If they seem quiet and unwilling to be open with you, it is most likely a mixture of bashfulness and fear of saying or doing something that might offend you.

• Trust your instincts. If you are uncomfortable about someone or a situation, speak up or enlist the aid of another volunteer.

• Let the guests carry the conversation. They often enjoy talking, not about themselves, but about current events, including religion and politics. It can be a lively exchange with good-natured teasing. Do not think that you must "fix their situation."

• Be a good listener. This means trying to understand what lies beneath the facts and information. It's hearing not only the details, but what all those details mean to the guest. Occasional clarifications, such as "you seemed so upset with him," or "you loved her very much," will assure the guest that you really are listening.

• Clarify any confusing information ("I didn't understand . . ."). Do the same with feelings ("How did you feel when that happened?"). The guest will gain confidence in you as a real support, even if just for the evening.

• Note body language. We cannot not communicate. So how a person moves around, facial expressions, and physical habits tell a lot about the person without your even speaking to the guest.

Ways to Reduce Tension

It's your night to provide shelter. You don't know why, but you can sense the tension among the guests. Not only do you want to avoid any possible conflict, but you want your guests to feel comfortable and at ease.

What can I do to make the guests feel welcome and avoid conflict?

• Understand where they have been that day. Life on the streets is tough. Beyond the dangers, your guests have dealt with people making unkind comments to them, passersby looking the other way, people telling them to move on, not knowing where or when they would find a place to use the bathroom. Anger, resentment, frustration can easily build up. In fact, when you consider what they live through before they come to you, it's amazing they are in any kind of good spirits at all. Understanding the "baggage" they bring in will help you deal with your guests more sensitively.

• As stated above, let them know what to expect. Remember that your guests go to a different congregation every night, and each congregation has a different procedure and set of rules. Clear expectations reduce tension.

• Remember that they are your guests, not your prisoners. Let them know how glad you are to see them. Tell them how much you hope their stay with you will be a pleasant one. The warm acceptance of them as your new friends will disarm most stressful and tense situations.

• Some guests attract us more than others. We enjoy seeing them. Try not to play favorites. Seek to speak to every guest, if only for a brief time. No one should feel neglected in the group. Be on the lookout for the guest(s) who may be alone. Offer to talk but respect his or her need to be silent and alone. By giving each guest some personal attention, you will gain the trust of the guests. They will respect you as a person who treats everyone fairly. This personal attention will help you reduce tension or resolve a conflict should it arise. Respecting you, those in dispute are more likely to listen to you than not.

• Solicit the advice of some guests whom you can trust. Generally, among the regular guests are some with good leadership skills. Often, they have a calming effect on the rest. Be careful to avoid putting them in authority. They will work best behind the scenes, mingling among the other guests.

• If the tension remains, meet it with a firm yet kind request that everyone try to get to bed as soon as possible. Rest is medicinal. Letting everyone know how difficult it must be for them to be on the streets doesn't hurt either. It assures them that you understand their plight, even though you are not homeless, and consequently are not upset by the stress and tension you sense among them.

The Importance of Safety and Security

As a host or hostess, your gift to your guests is the hospitality of a safe, secure night's rest—a respite from a life-style that is anything but safe and secure. This gift is provided in many ways: a smile, food, a warm room, a listening ear, a non-judgmental heart, a clean towel, a bar of soap, shaving cream.

At the same time, you do those things that ensure a safe, secure environment. This means that you create security in your facility. You designate clearly their shelter space. You know where your guests are at all times. You limit access to sensitive areas where important records and equipment are kept. You do not allow guests to come and go from the shelter during the night. You ask that all guests leave together in the morning.

You carry out rules that ensure everyone's security. For example, guests sleep more easily if they are assured that no one will be roaming around and rummaging through their belongings. You check safety factors, such as making sure the proper doors are locked or that there is nothing to trip over during a nighttime walk to the bathroom.

By taking care of such details you will create an atmosphere of trust. You will let them know that your security rules are for their protection as well. While it is important for you to trust the guests, it is also important for them to trust you. Should something be damaged or lost in a part of the building that is off-limits, you want to be able to defend each guest from any false charges. The rules about security do that.

An Awareness of Your Role

Running a shelter does not happen without planning and coordination. More than a few people are involved. Each has particular responsibilities. Sometimes those duties overlap, such as having two food servers, but always they should be clear.

Duties of a host or hostess vary from providing meals to driving a van to overseeing the clothing room to cleaning up. Samples B, C, and D in the Appendix contain illustrations of the kinds of jobs that are needed.

As a volunteer, it is important that you know your role and be faithful in fulfilling it. Not to do so will result in confusion and ultimately undermine the safety and care of the guests.

How to Work with Other Volunteers

The following guidelines will help you serve well with other volunteers:

• Don't overrule a decision of another volunteer. Consult with the person or the coordinator if you have a problem. Nothing undermines the spirit of cooperation more than an overzealous volunteer not working with the others as a team.

• If you do not have enough to do, offer to help others who may be busy. Or use the time just to visit with the guests. That free time can be invaluable for them, since few people take the time simply to listen to them. Since there are so many tasks that need to be done, hosts often have little time built in for personal conversation. Yet this remains the heart of the gift of hospitality.

• Generally, all the guests present particular needs. Some are better at dealing with them than others. Always be on the lookout for any "special needs" situation. For instance, the elderly person who may need help carrying a tray, the disabled person finding access to the bathroom, or the family with a baby that needs infant formula.

• Know what to do in any emergency. Know the proper procedures beforehand. If there are none, ask enough questions to know what is expected of you should an emergency arise. There are three kinds of emergencies: (1) building and maintenance, e.g., the heat goes off. Whom do I call? (2) medical, e.g., someone is choking. What do I do? (3) interpersonal, e.g., two guests are arguing. What next?

• Be punctual in arriving when you are scheduled. Every delay penalizes the guests. If you are unable to meet your commitment for the evening, arrange your own substitute or call the coordinator of volunteers.

• Offer to serve in any capacity, but identify your strengths. Know what you do best and what you enjoy. They may not be the same. For instance, as a welcome break, an accountant who is talented with details might want to do something that does not involve a lot of details.

• Accept the fact that you will make mistakes. You might say the wrong thing and offend. You might neglect a duty. You might look foolish. Cheer up! You are in familiar territory. Failure is the common denominator among the guests. Admit your mistake to those involved and learn from it.

• There is no correct way to be a host or hostess. Your talents and personality traits are unique. Develop your own personal style within the context of hospitality. You will be loved not only for what you do, but for who you are.

Knowing Who Makes Decisions

A well-run shelter will clearly define for every volunteer how decisions are made. Volunteers then need to work together as a team and trust one another to discuss an issue when decisions are required. It is important for the safety and security of the guests that this be done. Just as children can pit parents against each other, so guests may go from volunteer to volunteer to get a decision they want. Typically, most decisions can be delayed until you check with the proper person in charge. If there is a clear line of authority that is properly followed, the guests will be more at ease and less confused.

For instance, if a guest sees a drug store next to the church and wants to leave to buy some cold medicine, that situation should be covered in your rules. If not, then check with the shelter coordinator. To make that decision on your own, as easy as it sounds, might create a problem for another volunteer on another night who refuses a similar request.

Remember, in addition to the general policies of Room in the Inn, every congregation has its own rules and establishes its own way of making decisions. A volunteer needs to know this and to work within that framework. Ask questions about decision-making if no one tells you. A simple rule to keep in mind is: never claim authority to make a decision about which you are unclear or have doubts.

Remember, Room in the Inn is yours. No set of guidelines will apply to your situation every time. We are all learning together.

THE CONGREGATIONAL COORDINATOR

At Room in the Inn, each shelter is under the authority of a *congregational coordinator*. This person is responsible for all decisions at the shelter.

Selecting the Congregational Coordinator

When the decision is made to start a shelter, the first action will be to place someone in charge. This person is the congregational coordinator. The duties of the congregational coordinator are five-fold:

1. *Organization and coordination.* These responsibilities include all matters related to getting started and keeping the program going. Imagine all the details that must be taken care of to get under way, such as selection and approval of shelter space, transportation, food preparation, approval of budget, supplies, maintenance, and clean-up. Now, set down all those duties and develop a plan to accomplish them. A committee is helpful in organizing this. (Refer to sample B in the Appendix.)

2. *Recruitment and training of volunteers.* There are all kinds of ways to recruit hosts and hostesses. The key to success is to spread the word through bulletins, newsletters, and meetings. Once again, use your imagination. One coordinator developed a one-woman skit portraying the plight of a homeless young woman. Using this format helped overcome some of the road-

blocks to volunteering and helped others begin to identify with the impact that being homeless has on people.

Another coordinator hosted a dessert at the church for all interested persons. She formed her Giraffe Club—for those who "stick their necks out" for the homeless.

Once a group is recruited, develop a training workshop to explain the program. This meeting should include social agency people familiar with working with the homeless and your local organizing team. You may want to include some homeless people to tell their stories.

Topics to cover in a training meeting include:

- philosophy of Room in the Inn
- how the shelter is organized (policies/rules)
- homeless profile (national and local)
- various concerns: medical, mental illness, conflict, vandal-ism/theft, contagious diseases, emergencies (medical or health department personnel needed for this portion)
- housekeeping details (cooking, clean-up, driving, etc.)
- volunteer guidelines (see chapter 8)

The first workshop will take considerable time. Allow plenty of time for questions to dispel all anxieties and confusion. Once the program is under way, future meetings will be shorter and may deal with other topics, such as burn-out, making referrals, or listening skills.

3. *Supervising and scheduling of volunteers.* This will be an ongoing work that involves overseeing the volunteers. It includes schedul-ing, arranging for substitutes, handling any conflicts among them, and delegating the responsibilities for each night of shelter.

4. *Liaison.* The coordinator will serve as the liaison with those outside the shelter—for example, the social agencies, the down-town pick-up site, the media, the police, and the hospitals. He or she will also report to the pastor and/or the governing board of the congregation, representing the interests of the shelter and in turn, report back to the volunteers.

It is important that the coordinator clearly define with the gov-erning body of the congregation who will be the official spokesperson with the media at all times, but especially in the event of an emergency.

5. *On-call for any special activities or emergency.* This responsibility covers all others not noted above. It may include counseling a troubled guest, arranging to fix a broken water pipe, soothing the hurt feelings of a fellow church member, or planning for Christmas gifts. It is being available to help solve any problem that the volunteers on site cannot handle.

Summary

The role of the congregational coordinator is crucial to the success of the program. He or she is the focal point. Those members of the congregation not involved will expect to hear glowing reports of success and few problems. The volunteers will expect good organization and communication. The guests who come regularly will appreciate seeing some familiar face that they can count on.

The task of the congregational coordinator is not easy. Yet without a confident leader in this role, the program is doomed to fail. There may be nice facilities and plenty of interest and resources to begin. But these are not enough to start. It is such an important position, I would not recommend that a congregation participate unless there is such a person to assume these duties.

The good news, though, is that every congregation has someone who has these special gifts. They may not be so obvious when you first look. But look again. You can see so much more a second time.

THREE SNAPSHOTS

Number 42

He is Joe Montana. Down by three with two minutes to go, it's the Forty-Niners' last chance. Penned back at their own 15 with one time-out remaining, the Forty-Niners look to Montana once again to lead them.

All eyes are on him.

With a deliberateness coming from years of practice, he begins his routine. Calmly, he quiets the crowd, sets his line, barks out the signals, takes the snap and hands off to the second man through, who gains a tough seven yards. Quick to the line again, he brings his team together. A second play, again with the same results.

The crowd senses the moment. The clock is moving. There is no time for error. Everybody has to concentrate; everything has to be precise.

This time a pass play good for thirty-four yards, out of bounds, and another first down. The clock stops and he huddles his team.

The players can tell who's in charge. He looks at each of them, encouraging one, pushing at another.

Play by play, they march toward the goal line. With a mixture of short passes, quick bursts up the middle, and delayed draws, he has them on the twelve with thirty seconds remaining and the clock ticking. Time for only one more play.

He calls his own number. Taking the snap, he fakes to his tailback going right and then bootlegs around left end. The cornerback is the only one between him and the goal line, five yards away. Moments like this are left to one's instincts and natural abilities. Going full-speed, yet shifting ever so slightly to his left, he freezes the corner momentarily, and darts right into the end zone. Touchdown!

Just then, the telephone rang.

Looking back over my shoulder, I walked toward the phone. I was not being torn away from Monday Night Football. Nor was this same latent boyhood dream, although many men still imagine such feats. I was caught up in a drama unfolding in an empty parking lot in the middle of downtown Nashville, next door to our Room in the Inn office.

The scene was the creation of a master dramatist. There on the lot, with the parking stripes as yard lines, a solitary figure acted out this game and all of its characters in pantomime.

Standing alone, his short-cropped hair matted with patches of gray around the ears, he looked like one of our football heroes, the aging warrior. His red jersey draped evenly across shoulders that filled it even without pads. His legs were lean and graceful. Jeans and high-top Nikes completed his uniform.

The number on his back was 42, not the 16 of Frisco Joe, nor any of those famous numbers of sports lore like 3 or 7 or 44. His was a number for the forgotten athlete, one that nobody famous ever wore. Appropriately, he played that part.

For ten minutes he had my eyes and the eyes of other passersby riveted on him. We were no Super Bowl crowd, but we had the same intensity.

Every movement was true. The way he leaned over the center, the three-step drop, the bootleg. He would stay cool when the play was blown dead, yet he high-fived it with his running back after some tough yardage. He pointed his finger in the face of a casual receiver, snapping him back to attention. But he petted and coaxed his offensive line, knowing more than anyone how much he depended on them. When he scored on that bootleg and that last swift fake, he gave a thunderous spike and a raised fist in triumph.

I found myself clapping and shouting, "Awwright!"

It was a signature performance, seen by only a few. A masterpiece! And it was a performance by one of the forgotten of our world, one of the homeless.

Day after day, Number 42 spends his time acting out his routines. He is judged to be a danger neither to himself nor to others. It probably is a correct assumption. Thus, he finds himself on the streets, rather than in a mental health facility.

No doubt he knows football and some survival skills. But what else does he have in his bags on the street? Job skills? A family that wants to help? Medication to ease his trauma? A hidden artistic talent?

Left to himself, who is there to find out? While he flounders, we drive by and presume that some mental health professional is keeping tabs on him. Actually, it's more a hope, since we don't want to feel guilty about his being there. And he's not alone. Studies estimate that thirty to forty percent of the homeless population suffers from some mental illness.

Isn't something amiss here? Physically disabled and educable mentally disabled persons can be trained to care for themselves to a great extent. Yet they are not left completely on their own. They live in homes where they are loved and are placed in schools that meet their special needs. Some of our finest and most dedicated people care for them. We even celebrate them with the Special Olympics.

Why is the same not done for the mentally ill? Assessment of their needs may be more difficult to measure than physical ability or intelligence. Still, a disability is a disability.

Missions and shelters are not the answer in helping the mentally ill. It's time for us to assume responsibility again. We need to change our methods of the past twenty years. No longer can we simply let them out, tell them to take their medicine, check with the community-based mental health facility when there's trouble, and "don't worry, be happy."

"Not being a danger to themselves or to society" is no criterion for abandoning our duty to provide quality care and support for such a large segment of our population.

There are just too many people like Number 42, forgotten people living in a world that nobody sees, who deserve better.

Clayton

The mentally ill are not the only ones who deserve better. There's another large group that most people know as winos or bums.

Remember the tramp? He's been with us at least since the Depression. He may be at the lowest rung on the social ladder. There is no future more bleak than his.

I remember when I was a boy of nine or ten, about the time boys begin to explore the neighborhood beyond their own street. Several of us rode our bikes through a large vacant lot overgrown with weeds and debris. We came upon a group of men clustered around a fire in the middle of a clump of scraggly old trees we called "The Jungle."

We had seen them before but didn't know them. Most of the time they looked drunk. Often each was alone. We weren't sure it was safe to hang around them, especially when they were in a group. Were they armed? Were they dangerous? Were they criminals?

Quickly, we pedaled away to regroup and scheme. "Let's go back, hide, and throw rocks at them." One of us had a better idea. "Let's get some cherry bombs and, while they're sleeping, throw them in the middle of them."

"Yeah," we all chimed in! The thought of hurling lighted firecrackers at them excited us. We would pretend to be planes dropping bombs on the cities.

Bolstered by group pressure, we set off on our mission. Down the hill, over the hump, into the middle of the camp we rode screaming and yelling and firing our missiles. The sudden explosions roused even those in the deepest sleep. But we didn't wait around to see what happened. We couldn't get away fast enough.

We flew two or three other missions. Then it began to bother us. We didn't like what we were doing. It wasn't fun anymore. So we stopped.

Eventually, we got to know the men. They took us into their group, and we became their friends.

Once that happened, whatever happened to them affected us differently. There was the time Clayton was arrested. It must have been his hundredth time. This time, though, was different because it was the first time I witnessed it.

The policeman, who was the neighborhood's toughest cop, pulled up beside Clayton sprawled drunk on the street. He roughed him up and slung him into the back of the paddy wagon. I still remember the thud of his head hitting the metal wall. I also remember telling the officer rather cautiously, "He didn't hurt anybody."

I was relieved that the officer didn't arrest me, but I also knew Clayton didn't deserve such treatment. The policeman didn't know him as I did. If he had, I thought, he would have treated him better.

As I grew closer to Clayton, I began to understand something about human relationships. My initial fears and suspicions had disappeared in proportion to my knowledge of him. The more I knew, the less I feared.

Gordon Allport's classic text on prejudice, *The Nature of Prejudice,* supports this claim. He begins one chapter with the short scene of two men talking about a third.

One says to the other, "See that man over there. Well, I hate him."

The other man says, "But you don't know him."

The first man responds, "That's why I hate him."

People who are homeless so often are victims of our prejudgment. The tramp suffers from this. He belongs to the group that we most commonly associate with the homeless. But they are more than vagrants and bums. Each remains an individual with a particular story of his own.

Studies estimate that the chemically addicted comprise thirty to forty percent of the homeless. My experience is that there are even more because alcoholism and drug addiction run through every known category of the homeless. The chronic wino is only part of that number. Others include young men seeking employment, women with children, runaways, the elderly, Vietnam veterans, the mentally disabled, and the mentally ill (the so-called "dual diagnosis").

As we learn more and more about addictive personalities, there is reason to hope. Chemical addiction is a disease that can be controlled with treatment and ongoing peer group support. Such personalities can become clean and sober. Thus the tendency to write them off as wasted lives should lessen with each passing year.

Still that day seems far off, as alcohol and drug treatment remain too costly for most who need it. The few who do receive government assistance for treatment come out of the program with their sobriety but little else. Often their only choice is to return to the environment that they left and eventually to their old habits.

Families: Myth or Reality?

The mentally ill and the chemically addicted are only two of the groups found on the streets. There are others. If we take the time to know them, they will dispel our prejudices. And as more of our stereotypes disappear, we discover more and more new faces among the homeless.

Some of those faces belong to entire families.

Not just single individuals, but families. Homeless families. Is there any group that pulls and tugs at us more? Is there anything that is more the antithesis of the American dream? Picture a man and wife and three children piled into a 1972 Buick, pulling into an average American city. Their gas tank is on empty; they've just replaced the alternator with the last $100 they have; they are halfway to their destination; and they are hungry, tired, and hopeless. The thought that a family—a husband, wife, and children—would not have a permanent place to be together and experience all that a family should enjoy contradicts our notion of family life.

We may justify why the mentally ill or the chemically addicted fall through the cracks and end up on the streets. They are there because of the chronic nature of their sickness, or the lack of resources for adequate treatment and after-care, or the magnitude of the problem they present, or the unwillingness of some of them to accept help. But how do we account for families who are forced to live outdoors?

How is it that they can slip through our safety nets and be lost on the streets? Where are their extended families? Even if the extended circle of relatives and friends is unable to help, where is the school system when the children drop out of school? Or the state human services department when it first hears that a child is living on the street?

That children—even one child—end up living on the streets is outrageous. It is unconscionable in a society that purports to care for its children.

Consider, for instance, another problem that we have begun to address in our society—the problem of child abuse. We are educating ourselves more and more about child abuse. We are horrified that the problem is so widespread and has gone undetected for so many years. Victims are coming forth from every part of our community—the inner city as well as our wealthier suburbs—telling horror stories of years of abuse and repeated acts of cruelty by those entrusted with their care.

The outcry is loud and sustained to the extent that state legislatures and local law enforcement personnel are enacting sweeping reforms. Everyone realizes that we have ignored or been ignorant of a treacherous sickness that has left permanent scars on innocent children. And no one thinks that we are overreacting to the problem. Many wonder if we are strict enough in our vigilance and enforcement.

Why are children on the streets not also viewed as victims?

Isn't it abusive that children not have a clean, safe place to live and grow? Of course it is. It disturbs us. We may even want to point the finger of blame. But then, whom should we blame? Parents? Society? The government? The economy? Someone or something else?

A social worker reports that when she asked a group of homeless children to "play house," they did not play the way other children traditionally play. Ordinarily, boys and girls take on the roles of Daddy, Mommy, and the children. They live in a house and pretend to cook meals, clean house, repair the chair, or cut the grass. The children who were homeless "played like" they were going to the soup kitchen to eat, to the shelter to wash and sleep, and to the streets to spend the day and look for work.

That social worker paints a tragic and sad picture for us. It's troubling to think about what happens to a family that experiences this reality. We may not even understand how it could happen. We do know, though, that it just doesn't make sense that families have to "play house" like this in the real world.

But they do. And their existence on the streets is perhaps the greatest single proof that life in America is changing dramatically for an increasingly large portion of our working poor.

For families are relatively new to the streets. There still is a wide discrepancy over the numbers that are there. Skeptics claim homeless families are a myth created by homeless advocates to generate public sympathy and government funds.

Where there *is* public sympathy for the homeless, families as a group probably generate more compassion than any other group. And rightly so, since they contain the most innocent among us, our children. Appropriately, government funds seem to be targeted first at rescuing them.

Still, homeless families are no myth. Any shelter in any city will verify their existence. To write about their non-existence may lessen our sensitivity. It may also be a form of denial in the face of such a shocking revelation. Even so, isn't the existence of one family enough to raise an outcry?

Unfortunately, there are many more families "out there" than we are willing to admit. Those who suggest otherwise do not have hard facts, just observations. And they differ from mine.

What the skeptics fail to understand, I believe, is that families on the streets have a greater need to hide than a single man or woman. And they do so for their own protection. Parents who are homeless generally are as protective of their children as any other group of parents. Perhaps, even more so. They know what a wide assortment of personalities and situations there are in any gathering of the homeless. They want to keep much of that from a child's view. Suspicious, worried, and fearful, parents are extremely reluctant to have their children exposed to any further aspects of the harsh realities of living on the street.

Added to that is their own uncertainty of the local authorities' policies and procedures about child abuse and neglect. The possibility that those authorities might take their children from them because they are on the street causes great anxiety.

Not least is the question of their own embarrassment and shame and the indignity they suffer in front of the children whenever they have to beg for something to eat and a place to sleep. It's less humiliating to remain apart and, if they have one, to stay in their car.

That car is so important to them. It serves many purposes—shelter, safety, warmth, mobility, and independence. As long as they can maintain their car—and many do not—they still have some control in their life. To lose it means a further diminishing of the few remaining options left to them. To leave that car parked with everything they own in it and to go inside a shelter for the night is a great risk that many will not take, despite assurances that the car will not be vandalized. Also, if parents have lost everything but some clothes and a few other belongings, staying huddled together in their own car may be the last symbol they can cling to as a reminder of the life they once had or that they still hope to achieve.

Over the years, I have had many families refuse, at first, to come and sleep at Room in the Inn. They preferred instead the safety of their car over the dangers they feared existed in a shelter. These dangers are even more threatening when the family hopes to sleep together, but the shelter requires that the women and children sleep separately from the men. Who can blame them, considering that they are in a strange city and know no one whom they can trust?

There is another reason why identifying and counting homeless families is difficult. Sometimes a family will meet some new friends in a city. Often the family will be invited to stay with the new friends for a few days because of the children. Those few days offer the family a brief respite but do not end their homelessness. Their newfound friends may be on the brink of being homeless themselves. Still, they are willing to help. Perhaps they reason that two households can pool what little each has and live more economically. Such living arrangements, however, usually are short-term, often ending in misunderstandings and tension. Once more, the family is uprooted, and the streets become their home again.

I have suggested several reasons why there are significantly more families living on the streets than people realize. Why are there are so many? They were not so numerous two decades ago. In the seventies, the mentally ill were the new faces appearing on the streets. They had been released from mental institutions without community-based mental health services available to them. During the eighties, more and more entire families began showing up on the streets.

Several issues contributed. Nationwide, we voted for policies and supported practices such as cutting taxes for the rich, reducing expenditures in the social services, reducing federal housing assistance, shifting the balance of trade to ever-increasing deficits, maintaining a below-poverty-level minimum wage, modernizing production lines, closing factories, relocating industries, and employing cheaper foreign labor.

Put simply, many families were unable to cope with the pressures of a global economy.

Room in the Inn

As wages did not keep up with the cost of living, the working poor saw more and more of their income spent on heat, water, and food, while having to neglect their mortgage or rent, until all the forces combined to squeeze them into living out of their car—provided they had been able to keep up the payments.

In one respect, families who are homeless are not so different from the early pioneer families who struck out for new territory. Often they too had little except a horse and wagon and a few possessions. But they had the hope of finding some piece of land in this vast country and had the ability to live off it whenever they did so. Their ingenuity, determination, and drive gave rise to our American dream of having a home of our own. Yesterday's wagon trains are no longer. They have been replaced by today's "We Tote the Note" jalopies.

In another respect, homeless families today are vastly different. There is no land available. No houses that are affordable. No apartments for rent. It's as if a huge "No Vacancy" sign is hung at the city limits of our major cities. Meanwhile, our public housing officials bemoan the increasing size of the waiting lists for housing, and real estate agents watch the prices of apartments and houses rise and rise.

What's left then for housing? Substandard rental houses or apartments, partially condemned for various code violations. Second-rate trailer parks. Dilapidated hotels and motels.

Generally, all of these rent either daily or weekly—a nice convenience if one hasn't saved up enough for a month's rent. But such conveniences cost. Pro-rated over a month, daily/weekly rates always are more expensive. For example, in Nashville a weekly room in a boarding house with common kitchen privileges and a common bathroom charges $90 a week, while some one-bedroom apartments in the suburbs rent for $250-$350 a month.

When one considers that the available work for most of those who are homeless pays in the $4.00–$6.00 range with no benefits, the conclusion is obvious. Housing for the poor, unless subsidized, costs far more than the one-third portion of one's income that is considered the "safe" figure for keeping up a household.

While many families are unable to withstand the pressures of maintaining some semblance of home life and end up on the streets, still others have had their problems complicated by sepa-

ration and divorce. These fractured relationships cannot be cal-
culated when counting homeless families, except to project a further increase in the numbers of families that are showing up on
the streets. The result is that many women with children have
begun appearing on the streets, and many husbands and fathers
have shown up having abandoned their role as provider.

This final scene portrays the rupture that completes the total
breakdown of family life. Forced to live with nothing, husbands and wives turn inwardly toward each other hoping to
find some tiny shred of what they once shared together. But
faced with the inevitable loss of everything they worked for,
they now must confront the reality of their own failures and
frailty. Instead of finding support, they face the shame of their
cruelty or their inadequacy or their humiliation or their rejec-
tion. The reality is so overwhelming that they turn their heads
and walk away . . .

. . . And walk out onto the street . . .

WHO ARE
THE HOMELESS?

The mentally ill, the chemically addicted, entire families, single women with children . . . They all have no homes.

But they are not the only ones. The list gets longer as more and more other groups appear. Does anyone really know just how many groups there are?

Fortunately, there are reports available to provide an answer. Over the years, studies have revealed between ten and fifteen categories of persons who are homeless.

Our local task force on homelessness identified eleven categories:*

1. Substance abusers: older alcoholics who drink because of their past, and younger people who drink and "do drugs" because they see no future. This is the most visible part of the population.

2. Displaced workers: workers, both male and female, who are no longer employed because they lack the skills to get and keep jobs in today's market.

3. Single heads of households and intact families.

4. Youth and runaway teens: forced to leave home, unable to fit into current foster care systems, and almost always the victims of some form of abuse.

5. Elderly and physically handicapped: monthly checks too small to afford housing.

*(Metropolitan Development and Housing Agency Task Force on Homelessness, 1986, Nashville.)

6. Mentally handicapped: mentally ill and mentally handicapped and those borderline individuals not able to function fully in society.

7. Battered women: fleeing abusive situations.

8. Older non-elderly women: unskilled or no work history and no family; divorced or children have grown and left home.

9. Illegal aliens: unable to get work, but not deported or assisted by immigration bureau.

10. Ex-offenders: those given forty dollars, a set of new clothes, and a date to report to their parole officer, often ending up on the street if they cannot locate housing or employment.

11. Veterans: an increasing proportion of the whole.

How Many Are There?

How many homeless are there in the country? Statistics vary. Republicans claim 250,000, while Democrats claim 3,000,000. The truth probably lies in between. But the 1990 census figures are of no help.

The 1990 census figure estimated 228,000. A word about that.

Those who argued that the census would be unable to count everyone and consequently would grossly underestimate the actual figures saw their worst fears reported. They claim that the census data was flawed from the beginning. The first problem was the definition that the census itself used for the homeless. Essentially, the term referred to people sleeping in shelters or outdoors. At first glance, the term may seem comprehensive enough, but it is actually quite narrow and limiting.

That definition fails to take into account all those people who have no homes and yet were not counted on "S Night" (street and shelter night—the night the census count was taken). Some were those who were doubled up in the apartment of a friend or relative; those who were in jail, in motels, in emergency rooms, in mental hospitals, and other institutions that particular night; and those who may have been outdoors but were not counted.

The second problem with the census was its limited coverage. Despite our presumption that the entire United States would be counted, primarily the large urban centers were targeted. The rural areas were outside the scope of the census.

Third, there were not enough people to conduct the count. In addition, their instructions prohibited their looking into abandoned buildings, densely wooded areas (New York's Central Park was off limits), and parked automobiles.

One local expert, invited to consult with the Census Bureau as its principal investigator, concludes that the census count was a "colossal failure." Conducting the only national independent evaluation, Bill Friscics-Warren reports that even the GAO (General Accounting Office), the government's own monitoring agency, deems the effort a failure.

The complications of determining an accurate number demonstrate how difficult it is to gain an understanding of homelessness. It illustrates clearly that the more effort we make to understand the problem, the more subtleties and nuances there are that shade and color our perceptions.

Does Research Confirm Our Own Experience?

The past decade has produced a large number of articles and books, studies and statistics to help us discover the facts. This research is easily available.

My experience tends to simplify the data. The homeless are people who have the same needs that I have. A simple way of learning what their needs are is to remember what I myself need. I presume that whatever I need, they need.

If the homeless need whatever we need, our personal experience will tell us a lot. In all likelihood, their problems are overwhelming. No doubt they face the triad of basic needs that allows Americans to live independently—housing, employment, and transportation. Beneath those obvious ones are even greater needs. Abraham Maslow's hierarchy of needs can serve as a basic primer. We have basic needs of food, shelter, and clothing. We have psycho-social needs, such as the need for friendship, education, affirmation, self-esteem. We have spiritual needs, such as the need for God or the need to discover the meaning of life or our purpose in living. Beyond those needs, the homeless present issues around health care, education, job training, family, and community.

Through personal contact we recognize this more clearly. Our own experience gives us a glimpse of an individual's need in a far more intimate way than by simply reading some research. Personal knowledge is first-hand information, not second-hand data, however reliable and verifiable it may be.

Accurate research is vitally important, however, for it serves to underscore the insights that we gain from our one-to-one contact. In addition to supporting our own experiences, facts and studies on homelessness reveal its complexities and serve as data for public policy change. A combination of personal experience with the homeless and verifiable research on homelessness can be the basis for an informed citizenry to move our country toward a national will to eliminate it.

Personal experience allows us the opportunity to understand the complexities, develop more sensitivity, and seek solutions that are not simplistic. We realize that simply building more affordable housing is not the answer, although it is an absolute ingredient in the formula that will eliminate homelessness. We know that reformers, academicians, developers, and politicians at times secure monies for brick and mortar and then wipe their hands with a sense of satisfaction. Our personal experience convinces us that getting people permanently indoors is only the beginning of the solution.

Current research confirms this. For instance, the current debate in Congress about affordable housing and a guaranteed right to housing for every American is an issue that affects more than just the homeless. There is now a housing crisis. It is one of our three top domestic problems. More and more voices are calling for it to become part of our national agenda.

The October 1989 march on Washington demonstrated that the homeless are now included in a growing number of people demanding legislation for affordable housing. For the homeless, this movement means that they finally have allies. They can ride piggyback with a larger segment of Americans—the working poor, newly married, renters, and others—who are finding it increasingly difficult to purchase a home.

Another example: Current research indicates that many of the homeless have skills and talents. They are resourceful with a remarkable resiliency. My experience confirms this. It tells me that most would choose another way of living. If there is a way to get off the streets, most will explore it. If there are services or programs designed to assist them, eventually the network on the streets will broadcast it. As a rule, they will investigate every possible solution to their problems. They seek to discover a better way of life. Again, personal experience confirms this.

What Happens When They Have No Hope?

Often the homeless look as if they have no ambition, no goals, no hope, no plan of action, and no desire to change. At that point, some may have exhausted all the options available to them. They may not know any better way to solve their problems. They may have reached a point of resignation and see themselves as doomed to remain this way for the rest of their lives.

When that happens, no longer are we talking about living. We are dealing with people who are alive but seem dead. They have no more hope, no more dreams, no more purpose at all for living.

In a world so dark and bleak, Room in the Inn appears as a lighthouse. It may be only a tiny ray piercing the darkness. Still it shines forth. When dozens of those lights surround a city, there is even more light. A friend of mine is fond of saying, "There is no competition between lighthouses." People of faith throughout a region can unite around this one single way of sheltering the homeless, and no one need worry about petty issues that divide and separate people of religion.

When that happens, believe me, people who are otherwise left for dead can be revived.

CHAPTER TWELVE

LET'S SAY WE'LL TRY IT

How Do We Get Started in Our Community?

Be imaginative and creative. There are not a lot of experts in the shelter business. We are learning and discovering what works best as we go along. During our first year, no one knew what would happen, much less which leadership style would evolve. We were involved in crisis management. We did whatever it took to get people indoors.

I cannot stress this point enough. Room in the Inn began with a few churches believing it could be done, even if we did not know exactly how to do it. We believed we had enough ingenuity and common sense to find the way.

Had we had every detail worked out, we would never have begun. We had to take risks, although I did not believe them to be unreasonable or imprudent.

We were fortunate that people who were experienced in working with the homeless helped design Room in the Inn. Some were ministers and human service workers; others were people in business, education, government, homemaking; some were retired persons.

It was imperative that we be convinced that the concept could work. There was no one but ourselves to substantiate our claims. It had not been done before. But having run a shelter at Holy Name Church the previous winter, I was absolutely convinced the idea was possible.

Several assumptions began to emerge immediately:

1) Local congregations create in their own facilities shelters for the homeless. These shelters operate weekly on a rotating schedule during the winter months. Volunteers prepare and serve food there. The facility is a safe, warm place with at least a sink and toilet available.

2) Shelters need to be small in capacity—ideally, eight to twelve persons, but no more than twenty. The psychology of the group changes as it grows larger, creating the potential for more problems.

3) The homeless are "guests" for the evening in the local "host" congregation. Volunteers are asked to treat the guests as they would want to be treated.

4) Each local congregation is responsible for its own operation. How it structures itself is its own business.

5) Rules and procedures are kept at a minimum. Only the basic ones are needed, and they are the most obvious—for example, no drinking, drugs, weapons, verbal abuse, or violent behavior is acceptable.

Initially, we organized around these principles. Even now they remain the basis of Room in the Inn. These five original principles can serve as the basis for any other group seeking to organize.

Room in the Inn is a shelter model that is proven and works well. I keep insisting that such a shelter can be simple, because I hope that interested people will not be scared off by the magnitude of the problems of the homeless and the complications of finding solutions for them.

You must be very clear about the purpose of an emergency shelter in your church or synagogue. The primary objective is to provide safe, warm shelter and food to people on the street.

The task is simple: to keep people from freezing to death or being subjected to the nighttime violence of the streets. An evening's shelter will not solve the myriad problems the homeless face, but it does meet immediate human survival needs. And it helps break the chain of hopelessness.

To begin, a community needs some interested people who have a lot of imagination and are willing to take some risks. Such people may be associated with a local group of the Coalition for the Homeless or with an anti-hunger group or a housing advocacy group. A local church may have an active social justice group. The Salvation Army is another resource in identifying interested people.

Such persons then become the organizing group, a steering committee, that coordinates a community-wide program. It needs to recruit congregations; train volunteers; and coordinate the reception, interviewing, and placement of guests in the congregations each evening. In another place, an existing shelter such as the Salvation Army may be the agency to oversee the program. Whatever works best in each locale is encouraged.

In Nashville, a small group organized and developed the details. They took responsibility for getting Room in the Inn under way. The Salvation Army did the initial screening during the first year. It served as the pick-up site for the first two years, until we secured our own facility.

In time, a larger group assumed responsibility, consisting of a coordinator from each congregation. That group met monthly for the first year. As the number of congregations increased, the representatives elected a Steering Committee to oversee the program. Eventually the need arose for a small staff; and, in response to requests for donations, some staff members were hired. The Steering Committee later became the Board of Directors of Room in the Inn.

I'm Still Not Totally Convinced

Convincing people of the value of opening their doors to the homeless requires a combination of several characters at once. You need to be a preacher, salesperson, psychologist, lawyer, cheerleader, dreamer, thorn-in-the side, and friend.

I remember how often I found myself speaking to interested groups and assuring them that they would have very few problems. People just happen to be homeless, I noted. They were still quite lovable and had many wonderful qualities. Since the homeless knew that they were in houses of worship they would respect such property and not vandalize the buildings, I proclaimed. Give them a place that is warm and hospitable, I argued, and they would do everything to keep it that way. I knew this from personal experience at Holy Name.

But it is also true that problems can develop. People who are homeless are not perfect. And we shouldn't expect them to be.

I wanted so badly for the congregations to participate that I tended to dismiss the questions of safety and security, disease, and mental illness that were inherent in an undertaking of this nature. Realistically, I knew that they were there. I had encountered all of them in my own experience. But they had not deterred me. Problems only underscored how great the need was.

I believed that if others were willing to meet that need and open their doors, they would discover how important it is to do so. Then they would take the steps necessary to provide the best possible environment for their guests. Every time I had a chance to explain how a shelter worked, my emphasis was always on the need and how a shelter answers a great need. The problems were secondary.

I remember our first training workshop. The people who came were well aware of the need, but they wanted to prepare themselves for any and all problems. Every imaginable objection was raised. Our committee tried to anticipate all of them, but still some were overlooked. Primarily, we tried to counter the myths about shelters.

Answering the Myths About Shelters

1. Shelters are not brothels. You set your own rules. Single men and women sleep separately. Families and children are supervised.

2. Guests are not unruly. People who have been on their feet all day do not want to stay up all night. They want to sleep. Morning comes at 5:30 A.M.

3. Shelters are not taverns. No alcohol, drugs, or sometimes even smoking are permitted.

4. Shelters do not take up needed space. Churches and synagogues are among the most unused spaces in a community between the hours of 9:00 P.M. and 7:00 A.M.

5. Disease is not rampant. The common cold and other weather-related illnesses are present, yes. But hospitals are full of people who are more seriously ill, and every church and synagogue seeks to visit them.

Our training session addressed each of those misconceptions. The workshop seemed to allay the fears. Besides addressing the myths commonly associated with shelters, it included the director of the homeless clinic speaking about the various illnesses often found among the homeless and someone from the Salvation Army explaining the problems of coordinating a shelter. Then some practical tips were offered that would help reduce the potential for problems.

Since that initial workshop, we have learned a lot. We also have seen how congregations who have participated for several years keep wanting to improve the way that they serve the homeless.

The appendix includes some materials that will serve as examples of how some congregations have organized their Room in the Inn shelter. They may stimulate the imagination and help people visualize the program.

Summary

None of the information about beginning a shelter, especially the matters concerning mental illness or medical issues, can substitute for the specialized training or experience required to meet the variety of needs the homeless present. That special training is available and should be called upon when necessary. It is limited, however, to emergency situations and special problems. Meanwhile, the larger population drifts along, night after night, with no attention or relief.

Everyone recognizes that shelters, while necessary, are not the long-term solution to the homeless problem. Still, they are a beginning.

Check your local homeless shelters. Find out if there are enough shelter beds to meet the demand. In all probability, they are overcrowded and turn people away.

If that is true, then I offer you a challenge. Seek to start a shelter for at least some of them. You may not think that you can make a difference. But you can. Everyone can. There are too many people dying on our streets for you not to try.

PERSONAL REFLECTIONS

> "Always there remains this need to explain to each other that we are good. We all have a constant need to be reaffirmed. . . . The whole human race needs a yea, a large ceremonial pat on the back that says, 'Come on, come on. We can make it!' "
>
> —Corita Kent

In the acknowledgments, I mentioned the problem I faced in writing this manual. I knew that simply presenting the facts about operating a homeless shelter would not be enough of a spark to ignite in people a desire to start shelters throughout the community. I believe something else is required. What that "something" is everyone has to discover in his or her own way.

Up to this point, I have presented the *facts* about Room in the Inn. What follows is what I have *discovered*.

Give a Person a Fish . . .

After searching my mind to answer every possible objection that people have about Room in the Inn, I realize there still remains one more. This last one seems to be philosophical. It's what I call the "give a person a fish" argument. The maxim is: "If you give a man a fish, you feed him for a day. If you teach him how to fish, you feed him for a lifetime."

Simply put, some argue that Room in the Inn only gives a person a fish for the night. It doesn't seem to teach anything about lifetime survival. To use a popular expression about relationships, it "enables" people to remain in their dependency. It doesn't encourage self-help.

Other objections, such as the details, dangerous situations, and personal safety issues, can be answered factually. I chose to address them first. These objections are reasonable. In fact, every one of them, if resolved convincingly, may move you and your congregation to open a shelter. This "fish" argument usually comes later, after the others have been addressed. Perhaps this last objection will not surface until after you begin.

What happens is that, first, you begin. Things run smoothly, far better than you expected. There is pride about what you are doing. The homeless are grateful. Your hearts are touched. Many of your members are excited. You see results. You are pleased. You even get some notoriety . . . perhaps some new members . . . maybe an increase in the collection basket . . . a generous donor who remains anonymous. You may find yourself saying, "Why did we not consider this before?"

Once you start, it becomes difficult to stop. Some of your members now would never want to close your doors until homelessness is eliminated. They have no problems at all operating the shelter and will guarantee its continuation as long as they are so committed. But you have to remind them to take time to rest so as to avoid burn-out.

There are others who begin to think about what you are doing in the larger scheme of things. They have been dedicated to the shelter and supported it by volunteering. They are no longer frightened by the homeless. They can engage homeless persons in friendly conversation and feel relaxed around them. The homeless seem to "like" coming to them. They start to see some of the same familiar faces week after week.

But they begin to wonder, "What am I really doing for this person? How does our shelter help solve the real problems of the homeless? It seems like all we're doing is making them more dependent. You know the old saying, 'If you give a man a fish . . .' "

Now you face a more difficult dilemma. It isn't a question of whether you have the resources and skills to operate a shelter. You know you can do it. It is more fundamental than that. For example, when you decide to buy a car, you raise many questions: price, fuel efficiency, warranties, size, and so on until you have enough information to make a deal. One question you may fail to ask is whether you should even be driving a car. Maybe you should use mass transportation. Raising the question about whether a shelter promotes more dependency is to question the very idea of creating shelters at all. Don't they only "give a man a fish"?

This last objection cannot be explained with facts. It rests deep inside you as part of your value system. It reflects the way that you look at the world, your "world view."

I am not talking about provable statistics, prudent caution, and responsible organization. I am talking about what I believe and what you believe. About myself. About yourself. About people. About relationships. About life.

How do you answer the fish question? Is a shelter a co-dependent trap? Should you be doing other things for the homeless, such as advocating for better legislation and government monies to eliminate the problem? Or maybe your time would be better spent in creating some programs of self-help—job training, a job bank, a literacy class, an alcohol recovery class?

If you are so drawn to volunteer in some special area of need, take the lead. Create that piece of the puzzle that you see is missing. There is more than enough work for everyone to do. Remember, though, how much will be expected of you if you do. Using the fish analogy, people who know how to fish did not learn it overnight. They will tell you it's more than just baiting a hook and casting a line. They are forever learning more about the habits of fish, the best bait, water currents, weather factors, and so on. In short, teaching people how to fish may take years. If you have that level of commitment, the homeless will benefit greatly. In the meantime, please, don't destroy the shelter system. Why? Here are some observations:

1. Until there is a national will to eliminate homelessness, shelters still are needed. Shelters will disappear when homelessness ends. Presently, there is no end in sight. The skeptics argue that shelters should be closed to force people to make it on their own. In effect, they argue that shelters create homelessness, which is the equivalent of saying hospital emergency rooms create emergencies.

2. What do the homeless do while you design the programs for

self-help? The fishing maxim about self-help always seems to be presented as an either/or rather than a both/and proposition. It suggests that instead of operating a shelter, you ought to be using your talents and resources to create self-help programs. Why not do both? Let the second objective grow out of the gathering of the ten to twelve individuals you welcome as guests. Our history at Room in the Inn is precisely that. Supplemental programs have grown out of our understanding that simply giving people a place to stay may help them if only for the night.

3. Still, do not underestimate what you do that night. If designed around the concept of hospitality where people are welcomed as guests, a shelter does more than you think. It is more than food and shelter for the evening. A lot of teaching is going on without your even noticing it. For example, you and your shelter are communicating:

- respect for one another rather than cruelty and abuse
- interracial harmony rather than racism
- kindness as a weapon rather than knives and guns
- unconditional love rather than controlling behavior
- disciplined rather than uninhibited choices
- a sense of order rather than chaos
- living according to a schedule rather than aimlessness
- self-acceptance rather than shame
- believing and hoping rather than giving up on life
- the use of words of kindness rather than words of hatred
- caring by example rather than by words only
- fair rather than arbitrary and capricious decisions
- safety and security rather than danger
- consistent rather than compulsive ways of behavior
- reasoned thinking rather than emotional reactions

Anyone who teaches knows that what people learn cannot be measured completely. Parents understand that for eighteen years the consistent message to their children that they are lovable is all the children have to hang on to when they leave home. Parents hope they have conveyed it well enough that their children will become self-reliant, act responsibly, and pass on the same message to their children.

At first glance, Room in the Inn looks as if it only gives a person a fish. Look again. It also teaches people how to fish. The consistent messages that are taught night after night have the power to help people begin to feel better about themselves. Each shelter can offer the spiritual energy to help people learn how to live a lifetime with others in good relationships.

You might not realize all that is happening, because you only operate once a week. Remember that you are part of a huge network of shelters that provide these same messages nightly. Together, you bring a sense of stability and calm to the guests each evening. For many it's the start on the road to more independent living.

All you might see on your congregation's particular night is the serving of a meal and friendly conversation. But look again. Notice that familiar face week after week. See if there is any slight change in that face. Does he seem to take better care of himself? Does she seem more at ease? Is he smiling more? Is she speaking about a future? Are they confiding in you as a friend whom they trust? Is there any sparkle returning to their eyes? Are they coming back to life? In short, can you believe that something good is happening in their lives even if you cannot prove it?

4. Room in the Inn is organized around the principle of hospitality. Everyone is welcomed as a guest. This is your ideal. Yet not every shelter in this nation operates with the same set of principles. People who are homeless can tell horror stories about the violence and abuse they have experienced in shelters. All you need to do is listen. Such violence usually occurs when people are devalued and demeaned, blamed and ridiculed. When shelters become too large in size, when staff is neither secure nor adequately trained, when the stronger ones among the homeless are allowed to overpower the weak by physical force or intimidation, when services such as food or clothing or showers are doled out without any apparent care or concern, then a dangerous and violent atmosphere full of suspicion and mistrust is created. One of the first lessons you will teach is that your shelter is different. The guests will know it without your saying it.

5. That Room in the Inn is an inter-faith effort means that the homeless are exposed to the widest range of religious traditions. From the more hierarchical churches to the more independent ones, as well as to other, non-Christian congregations, the home-

less come as guests and leave with a better appreciation of the broad range of expressions that exist about God and service to neighbor. When every shelter provides the same gift of hospitality, there is no cause given for any guest to make the claim that Catholics are better than Jews or Baptists better than United Methodists. Religious pluralism is respected without a sermon ever being preached.

6. Room in the Inn is not about goal-setting but about the gathering of people. Setting goals may occur when people get together; yet you do not have permission to do that for another person unless the person gives you permission. You can only invite people to stay with you for a while. That simple gathering of hosts and guests may lead to their wanting to change some things about their lives and choose a new direction.

To return to the fishing maxim for a lesson, I might have the ability to teach someone to fish for a lifetime. Still, it can't be forced. That person might not want to learn. I believe, though, that she may be willing to listen if she sees me as someone who cares. What can I do to show that I care? Feed her a meal of fish for the evening with no hook attached. Let her be free to accept my friendship or not.

I can't prove any of the above from statistics. It's just the way I believe people want to be treated, because it's the way I've always wanted to be treated.

Empowerment

I have discovered something else that is difficult to prove. It's what the experts in the human services call "empowerment."

Every modern textbook on human behavior stresses how important it is to help people help themselves—to teach people how to fish. From the day-care teacher's toilet training techniques to the therapist's couch, people need to be empowered with the attitudes and abilities to take care of themselves, not to be taken care of.

What is this power anyway? The power of self-esteem? The power of self-reliance and self-assurance? The power of self-determination? The power to live freely and independently?

We hope so. In fact, we want that for everyone, but can we ever be sure? The subtleties of human interaction are so tricky. We are fond of speaking about our agenda and those "hidden agendas" of others. There may be "hidden agendas" even in our notion of empowerment. The language itself might veil a hidden need we have as "helpers" to control those being helped. Empowerment could mean that I, as the one with power, want to bestow that power benevolently on another.

What then do I mean when I say I want to empower people? Does it mean that I want them to learn to be like I am? Does it mean that they must embrace my standards of living? Do they have to think the way I do about God? About America? About politics? About family values? About life?

For instance, there are certain practices and beliefs in our culture that we take for granted, but others may not. A report on public radio states that people in Mexico see a meal as an occasion to build closer family relationships and community, not as a place to conduct business, which a meal often becomes in our culture. A couple from Germany tell me that the first thing Americans ask upon meeting them is, "What do you do?" suggesting that we value people by what they do, rather than by who they are.

Empowerment means helping people discover how important they are—in themselves, independently of others. It also means helping them recognize within themselves the talents and abilities that are unique to them and encouraging them to develop those gifts in relationship with others. This is no easy feat. Messages all around us remind us that we are being evaluated constantly according to a set of standards. Think of the measurements that we use in our culture to evaluate people. We are compared to our brothers or sisters, to our friends, our classmates, our neighbors, our business associates, our peers. We have standards about decency, style, manners, taste, success, civic duty, patriotism, and religion. In addition, our personal appearance is a point of comparison, sometimes too painfully, because we are overweight, too thin, unattractive, out of style, clumsy, ugly, deformed, disfigured, or impaired with visual, hearing, or speech problems. The old saying is true that "comparisons are odious."

We learn early what is expected of us. Generally, the message is to measure up—to something or someone. Conformity becomes the norm. Nonconformity means abnormality, with penalties and punishments attached. Before too long, easily by the end of adolescence, we know whether or not we are successful at conforming. We may even have the scars to prove it.

As we enter young adulthood, life becomes a series of adjustments to what others expect of us and, at the same time, a tussle within ourselves to follow our own dream. We seek a balance that allows us to live freely and with enthusiasm. Some of us are better than others at striking this balance. In the end we see the wisdom of our ways, and the story of our life will tell how well we lived our dream and still preserved and developed some cherished relationships.

Those who are homeless often have lost in love and given up on their dreams. Empowering them means helping them dream again by loving them as they are, not as we want them to be.

Remember, though, that homeless persons walk on a street filled with empty promises. It doesn't take long for them to be skeptical about our concern because most people pass them shouting obscenities out the car window or harboring secret resentments. All our talk about empowerment means little if they see no action—if there are no organizations or agencies in our communities that can offer them another chance. Empowerment means more than training and rehabilitation programs. Computers can teach them, and they can learn skills to guarantee some employment. To empower them also means harnessing the energies of hundreds of compassionate people throughout our communities to be the heart and soul of those programs, thus avoiding the creation of another uncaring bureaucracy.

When all that energy is harnessed, then empowerment takes on even greater meaning. Dr. Barry Lee, a former sociology professor at Vanderbilt University, conducted a poll of Nashvillians regarding their feelings about the homeless. He reported that 82 percent of the people interviewed "overwhelmingly favor providing more public services for the city's homeless" (*Tennessean,* November 24, 1987, p. 1). "I think the real litmus test is that . . . a majority of the respondents said they'd be willing to increase taxes if that's what it took," he said in a Nashville *Banner* story (November 19, 1987, p. A-12). In a private conversation, he told me that most of the persons he interviewed had attributed their caring attitude to some personal contact with at least one homeless person. Personal contact led to more understanding.

Ten years ago, fewer than a dozen people, representing a few organizations, sat around a table in Nashville and called themselves the local Coalition for the Homeless. Today, forty to fifty people meet monthly representing more than two dozen agencies and groups. Ten years ago, the Union Mission and the Salvation Army were the only bastions of help on the streets of Nashville. Today, there is involvement from many sectors. First came the ecumenical and inter-faith projects such as soup kitchens and shelters. Next came the city government's participation in creating a downtown clinic and a service center; then came the private sector, willing to invest in low-cost housing. Finally, the banks have joined in a partnership with non-profit organizations to create 170 new apartments, the first housing units ever designed in the city specifically for the homeless population.

The cost of all these services would now be in the millions, if not for the voluntary efforts of so many individuals and groups. Yet the actual cash outlay remains only a fraction of those estimates. The problem still is not solved by any means. But these efforts have helped in a most cost-effective way to move scores of people into permanent housing, provide support to hundreds of others, and keep the numbers of homeless from rising yearly.

All this would not have happened ten years ago. Why? Because ordinary people did not believe they could do anything about a seemingly insurmountable problem. They were not empowered.

Once again, we have to take a second look—this time at the notion of empowerment. Although I cannot prove it, I have discovered that empowerment of the homeless does not include just the homeless. Empowerment also means that a local citizenry can realize the imagination and ability it has within itself to solve its own problems and then can find the courage to do it.

Homestead

It is the great adventure in settling the West. The Homestead Act of the late 1800s gave everyone who wanted it a chance to claim a piece of land and build a home. To stake a claim and create a homestead was the incentive that led thousands of people to take a risk. It was the "venture capital" needed to open up new territory. With the coming of the settlers came commerce, trade, banking, manufacturing, and industry. People became neighbors; schools and houses of worship were established; libraries and hospitals were added; communities were formed.

Not being a historian, I wonder what the thinking was that led our nation literally to "give away" land. Did everyone believe somehow that people deserved a chance to create a life for themselves with no strings attached? As so often happens, was there self-interest involved? Was the Homestead Act in the best interest of our country?

Ultimately, I believe the thinking prevailed that it *was* in our best interest. And so the West was won.

Today, the idea of government "give-aways" borders on governmental heresy. Programs that offer some monetary relief have been under siege since the War on Poverty in the 1960s. The popular argument that has supported the policies of the 1980s has been to cut out the free lunch so people will be forced to work for what they get. Both presidential platforms in 1992 reflect a work-fare view. Such thinking inevitably remains simplistic, never taking into account two primary groups: (1) most people who are receiving government assistance are women with children, the elderly, and the disabled, not "able-bodied" males; and their entire yearly benefits still keep them below the poverty line; (2) the majority of those living in government-defined "poverty" receive no government assistance whatsoever; this remains one of our best-kept secrets, the so-called "working poor."

The only acceptable premise that prevails today is the thinking that government should not give away anything except in one instance—to those who are "truly needy." But the problem becomes determining what is a true need and then deciding who has it.

Scores of research documents verify what we need to live a life of fulfillment. As a government, we pick and choose from that data what we want to designate and fund as priority. On the one hand, the need to be reassured about national security results in a philosophy of "overkill" regarding our spending on weapons; everyone knows there are more than enough weapons around to defend ourselves. On the other hand, there are not enough food policies and programs to eliminate hunger in America. Juxtaposing these two examples tells me that, as a nation, we are quite clear in assuring hungry people that they truly need to be defended from outside aggression. If you were to ask them, however, they just might tell you they would rather be dead than live on the edge of starvation.

Besides the problem of determining our true needs, the question arises, "Who determines those who are truly needy?" Bureaucracies are filled with sets of standards and procedures that become a maze through which many will not travel. Poor people refer to it as being put into the shuffle—depersonalized slots filled with hours of waiting so they can be "verified" and "certified" as truly needy. Long lines, reminiscent of the Depression, stand waiting for cheese at a government give-away site. "Take a number," usually a high one indicating a long wait, says a sign at the local food stamps office and Social Security office. A quick check at any of these sites reveals what we would expect: minorities, elderly, women with children, sick people, people with disabilities, and everyone else living on the edge, patiently waiting.

But recently, another group has begun appearing, especially at unemployment offices, seeking compensation. In this group are those who may never have thought they would lose their job, because they were in the more secure middle class. Factory workers, technicians, analysts, middle management personnel— people with college and/or professional training. They are showing up to claim their benefits and are desperate for work.

Probably nowhere is this more dramatized than in Homestead, Florida, after Hurricane Andrew created the single worst disaster in the history of America. Tens of thousands of people were displaced and became homeless overnight followed by additional thousands on the Hawaiian island of Kauai, after Hurricane Iniki.

As a nation, we were shocked at the wreckage. Immediately, volunteers and businesses from across the country started sending money and supplies; but clearly the need was greater than what caring people could provide. Eventually, the government began to respond. As of this writing, the government has created a new dole. But no one objects to the give-away: the people in Homestead and Hawaii are truly needy.

The homeless are no different. Though not as visible, they have needs far more difficult to meet than the victims of a hurricane. Still, the homeless do not strike us as truly needy. Somehow their condition remains their fault. So many people remain convinced that homelessness could have been avoided. I have discovered at Room in the Inn that it's hard for me to prove otherwise, statistics and studies notwithstanding. I've come to believe that such thinking might never change—until and unless it's in our self-interest as a nation to do so, as we discovered by the Homestead Act years ago and in Homestead, Florida, just yesterday.

Another Look at the Christmas Story

I have discoverd something else about Room in the Inn that is not based on any facts, but is contained in its very name.

More than thirty years ago, theologian H. Richard Niebuhr, in his classic *Christ and Culture*, raised one of the toughest questions facing Christianity: Is Jesus Christ relevant to the situations we experience, the culture of our time?

It seems to be a timely question even now. Some say that our culture has entered a post-Christian era. They argue that Christians might still be holding on to their Christian symbols, perhaps best illustrated by church buildings, but their hearts are empty and void of Christian life. Some bland imitation, called "secular religion," is all that's left.

Others may delight over such a turn of events. They would contend that our culture from 1776 onward was never meant to be Christian. A plurality of religious expressions was the intent of the founders of our country, and no establishment of any particular religion was allowed.

More recently, the late John McKenzie, after a career of more than forty years of biblical scholarship, argued quite candidly in *The Civilization of Christianity* that "there is a deadly and irreconcilable opposition between western [culture] and Christianity, and that one of them must destroy the other." Christianity, he said, is at odds with a culture that seeks to twist or soften or evade its basic teachings.

As serious as this problem may be for Christianity in our mod-

97

ern world, it's not new. It's as old as the Bible itself, as old as the human race.

Whether or not Jesus Christ is relevant anymore to our culture may best be answered by the attention that each of us gives to the celebration of Christmas. Taking it at face value, Christmas is a confusing mixture of images and messages. At one and the same time, it is a great merchandising season, a winter holiday break from school or some other responsibility, and a religious holy day. A local newspaper ad captured the mix well: "Wishing you Christmas joy! Store hours: 9 A.M.–9 P.M." Both the secular and the sacred compete for our attention. And it's precisely because of this struggle that Christmas has so much staying power.

We know how we love to create stories, and we organize ourselves around them. These stories are cause for celebration and remembrance. They evoke mystery and wonder, joy and grief, dreams and aspirations.

Christmas is such a story. Its primary expression, enshrined in the sacred writings and sanctioned through the years of Christian tradition, is the lovely message of God revealing divine life to the world in the form of a new baby. It captivates us with its simplicity, yet is forever rich in meaning and detail.

Theologian John Shea describes it this way: "The story line begins with the concept of a virgin, for no human power can bring God into the world. God comes of his own accord, a free and gracious act of union. Once born, the child is placed in a manger, a feeding trough. . . . The God who freely enters now freely gives himself as food for the world."

Shea goes on to say there are those who push and those who get pushed. There are those who decree a census and those who must travel to register. The parents and child are outcasts; they are travelers; there is no room in the inn. This is not the stuff of sentiment and romance but the cruel facts of poverty. This is the same child who later has no place to lay his head and in the end stretches out his arms on a criminal's cross. In the powerlessness of this scene, Shea writes, we enter a world of reversal where wealth and poverty, power and weakness are overturned. Can a child born in a stable be the savior of the world? Can what is weak in ourselves and in the world be the bearer of a blessing?

From the beginning, this child is to be a sign of contradiction.

For some (the magi) he is a heavenly sign of God's revelation; for others (Herod) he is a threat to evil ways.

Shea concludes that later Christology stressed that the act of redemption was the death of Jesus, although some speculated that redemption occurred at the moment the Son of God took on a human nature. In actuality, the great act of sacrificial love takes place on Calvary. Still, there are more conversion stories associated with Christmas than with Good Friday. The birth narratives, he says, are in miniature what the entire Gospel story is about: invitations to change our hearts, to be converted ("Does Jesus Believe in Santa Claus?" *U. S. Catholic*, December 1980, pp. 6-13).

To what extent, then, does this story that invites us to conversion have relevance in our life today? Do we see ourselves in any way in the story? Perhaps a fresh interpretation is needed that will serve as an answer to the relevance of Jesus in our culture. And the dramatic phrase, "there was no room in the inn," may be the clue.

No room in the inn. The parallels between our cities and Bethlehem seem clear. Strangers come into the city, looking for a night's lodging. Even a census is taken. Back alleys where the dogs and cats roam for food are the sleeping quarters for many.

Imagine being in a strange city where you know no one. You are penniless, with only the clothes you have on and a small bag. You do not feel safe to use your own name, only a first name at best. You sleep, whenever you can, always with one eye open. You have no access to medical care, education, job training.

Into this world, this demented inn, in which there is absolutely no room for Him at all, Christ has come uninvited. But because He cannot be at home in it, because He is out of place in it, His place is with those others for whom there is no room. His place is with those who do not belong, who are rejected by power because they are regarded as weak, those who are discredited, who are denied the status of persons, who are tortured, bombed, and exterminated. With those for whom there is no room, Christ is present in the world. He is mysteriously present in those for whom there seems to be nothing but the world at its worst. . . . It is in these that He hides Himself, for whom there in no room.

—Thomas Merton

Originally, Jesus, the Messiah, came as a stranger. Who recognized him? Only those who had such vision to believe that God is revealed in the stranger among them. That same Christmas story is retold in your shelter each night, and you can see that vision unfold.

The story can also be rewritten. A Christmas play was held at a local school. All the important parts were given to the smartest students in class. The smartest girl was given the part of Mary, and the smartest boy was given the part of Joseph. The next smartest group played the part of the Wise Men; then the next group the part of the angels. The shepherds' parts were assigned to the next group. There was really only one bad part, and it was given to the least gifted student in class. That part was the role of the Innkeeper.

As the day of the play approached, the boy who was to play the Innkeeper began to worry more and more. He loved the child Jesus, and could not imagine having to tell Mary and Joseph there was no room in his inn. "What am I going to do?" he thought.

Finally, it was curtain time. Parents, relatives, and friends packed the auditorium. They proudly watched the story unfold with their children playing such important roles.

Meanwhile, the Innkeeper was nervous and worried backstage. He felt the pressure mounting as Mary and Joseph approached. And he didn't know what to do.

When Mary and Joseph knocked, suddenly he threw open the doors and exclaimed, "Come on in, I've been expecting you!"

With that, the crowd cheered and clapped and the play came to an end. And the little Innkeeper was the star of the show.

Like the little Innkeeper, Room in the Inn offers your congregation an opportunity to rewrite the Christmas story. Your shelter can reverse that ancient sin by welcoming today's strangers in your midst.

Not only is the Christmas story about welcoming strangers as if we were welcoming the Lord, it is also about whether or not we recognize the need to create space in our own lives for God. To that extent, it may be no different from our beginnings in the book of Genesis, when we chose to go it alone. There Adam and Eve are portrayed as hiding themselves from God. That story describes God as looking for them, calling out, "Where are you?" Later, when the time finally comes for God to enter the world, be enfleshed in humanity, there is no room in the inn—only room among the animals.

Maybe Jesus is not relevant to our culture because we have no need of him. We need to ask ourselves this question: "Do I need God? Am I so self-sufficient, or am I so busy, or is my life filled with so much clutter that there is no room in the only inn that my spirit knows—the interior thoughts and desires of my mind and heart?"

And we might remember that there seems to be the element of surprise in all this too. How and when God chooses to come into our lives, how that happens, often amazes us. A young man working with his high school class as a volunteer at a soup kitchen writes about it this way:

> The first Saturday of each month students make lunch for the homeless at Holy Name Catholic Church (Loaves and Fishes). You get a good look at the underprivileged there. For some, it's the first time in a while they've had food. It makes you thankful. The people shake your hands. It really gets you thinking about yourself. You think you'll always have enough money to do the things you want to do and think you can't live any other life-style. But there are others living worse and surviving only on faith. *You're humbled a bit.*

Spiritual writers for centuries have written that whenever we encounter the true God, we are humbled. From Moses' encounter at the burning bush, to the shepherds and magi kneeling in adoration at the Bethlehem stable, to Paul's conversion on the road to Damascus, the scriptures tell the story of people falling on their knees out of a sense of humility.

Let's be clear about our terms: humility, not humiliation. Whatever, whoever causes us to become "humbled a bit," not humiliated, is of God.

Making room in your life for all those people and circumstances that make you humble a bit is to make room for God. Creating space for the homeless in your shelter can be the occasion for such experiences.

This too I cannot prove. But I believe it happens.

A Final Word

We do not know what the coming years will bring. Two issues loom on the horizon: economic turmoil and a health care crisis. Creating a shelter at this time for the homeless may be the first step congregations take in meeting the need to establish more permanent space—even for their own members—for newly displaced workers and those unable to gain access to health and respite care. Already there is an urgency to meet the needs of the sick and dying, especially those suffering from AIDS. The details of operating a shelter are applicable to any group one may choose to serve—the homeless, the elderly, AIDS sufferers, migrant workers, ex-offenders, the mentally disabled, Alzheimer's victims, and on and on.

One final time, my appeal is to take a second look around you. Look again at those in need, look again at the unused space at your place of worship, and see if you can match your wits against all the opposition that would say, "It's not possible." Then, I challenge you to commit your imagination and your will to a great cause, the cause of rewriting the original story of there being no room in the inn.

IN MEMORIAM
(1982–1992)

The following persons have died trying to survive on the streets of Nashville. Some died of natural causes, some by accidents, and some by violence. Charles Platt was homeless at the time of his death, but he died of a seizure during the early morning hours on January 3, 1991, while sleeping in one of our church shelters, the only person at this time who has died in our midst. Chuck Cates, one of our guests, penned these verses shortly before he was murdered on April 3, 1990, two days after Room in the Inn closed for the winter. He had planned to return to Florida in a few days.

> I knelt to pray when day was done,
> I prayed, O Lord, bless everyone.
> Lift from the deadened heart the pain,
> And let the sick be well again.
>
> But never once did I go to see
> The sick man next door to me,
> Or try to lift the heavy load
> Of any brother along the road.
>
> But once again when day was done
> I prayed, O Lord, bless everyone.
> And then one day as I knelt to pray
> There came a voice that seemed to say,
> "Pause, hypocrite, before you pray!
> Who have you tried to bless today?"

God's greatest blessings always go
By hands that serve him here below.

And then I bowed my head and cried
Forgive me God for I have lied.
But if you'll let me live another day,
I'll try to live the way I pray.

—Charles Cates

David Harding
Thomas S. Elliott
Lannie Slayman
Ray Sanchez
Michael Blair
Vincent Rowan
Franklin "Mitch" Mitchell
Sidney Woods
Robert Hindman
Charles Platt
Sheila Gutierez
Mary Ann Sheets
Dan Pichotte
Albert "Preacher" Warrick
Anthony Weatherly
David Steward
Charles Douglas Rexrode
Grady Hanks
Charles "Chuck" Cates
Billy Joyner
Robert Adams
George "Elmo" Watkins
Anthony Hughes
Franklin Daley
Charles Kelley
_____ Fernandez
William Blair
Ricky McLemore
Kevin Stanford
Charles Shelton
E. L. Woodham

Chelsey Williams
Ray Zimmerman
Carol Kessler
Flavio Nunez
Junior Hallum
Richard Watson
Richard Bohanon, Jr.
James Deering
Rollin T. Roy
Frank Whisett
Robert Green
James C. Matheney
Herbert Nichols
Mike Murphy
Donald Pogue
William Wells
R. J. Ingram
Bonnie Ramsey
Unknown 3/10/90
Unknown 5/23/90
Hobert Giles, Jr.
Gordon Lambert
William Lines
William Edgar Lowery
Harvey Neese
Bonnie Parker
Ronald Watson
Charles West
"Mad Dog"
Mad Dog's wife
John Chadwell

APPENDIX

SAMPLE A:
WHAT IS A MEDICAL EMERGENCY?

A medical emergency is defined as a case of life-or-death illness or injury, acute distress, or great pain where the patient must be placed under professional care as quickly as possible. All such emergencies are taken to the nearest hospital or the hospital of your choice.

WHAT IS A PARAMEDIC?

The paramedic staffs the ambulance service vehicles and is highly trained and certified by the state as a cardiac rescue technician. He or she is capable of evaluating and treating a medical emergency.

WHEN MEDIC UNIT ARRIVES

Have someone guide the paramedic to the patient.
Keep bystanders and on-lookers away from the patient.
Make sure the area is well lighted.
The paramedic sometimes needs to give medications or perform certain tests on the patient before the patient can be safely transported to the hospital. Questions asked by the paramedic are important. Do not disturb or shout at the paramedics when they are performing their duties. No more than one or two people will be allowed to ride with the patient to the hospital.

Appendix

If the paramedic determines the patient does not require emergency transportation, a supervisor will be contacted. You may be requested to take alternative transportation. Some of the alternative transportations that we suggest are:

1. A private automobile
2. A taxicab
3. A private ambulance. Private ambulance companies are listed in the yellow pages of the telephone book.

CALL FOR A PRIVATE AMBULANCE

If the patient is not an emergency case, call for a private ambulance. The Fire Department Ambulance Service will not transport patients to:

1. Doctors' offices or medical centers
2. Any state mental hospital
3. Neighborhood emergency clinics

WHEN YOU NEED A MEDIC UNIT

Make sure you have a true emergency.

Call 911 or your local emergency number. Speak slowly and calmly.

Give the ambulance dispatcher this information:

1. Nature of emergency (what is wrong with the patient or patients).
2. Exact location of patient (address, apartment number, cross street).
3. Your name and telephone number (you are calling from).
4. Let children call for an ambulance only as a last resort.

If the patient is unruly or violent, call the police also at 911.

If you are reporting a traffic accident, give the following information:

1. Exact location of the accident
2. Number of patients
3. Number of vehicles involved
4. Type of vehicles involved, if known

Don't panic or shout.

Don't hang the telephone up until told to do so.

Send someone to signal your location to the unit.

SAMPLE B:
ROOM IN THE INN PROCEDURES GUIDE

EMERGENCY NUMBERS:

Coordinator's number: _____
Room in the Inn building: _____

The first-aid kit is in the small bathroom off the elders' conference room—you have a key on the key chain to unlock that door.

In case of snow during the night: Call Coordinator: _____
1. All volunteers should arrive at the church building by 7:00.
2. The evening driver should leave at 7:00 to go to the Room in the Inn building at _____ to pick up 14 guests, 14 blankets and towels. When you leave the van unattended, lock it. Check in with the worker in charge who will give you a list of guests and make sure the right guests get on the van.
3. Meanwhile, hosts/hostesses should prepare for the guests' arrival:
   • Place plastic-covered mattresses on the floor against the walls. Put a single fitted sheet on each.
   • Place host/hostesses mattress near door to hallway in case guests should need assistance during night. Put your belongings on these before the guests arrive so they will be reserved for you.
   • Prepare food. It should be waiting for you in the kitchen. You will need to plug in the coffee pot for hot water and arrange instant *decaf* coffee, cocoa, sugar, artificial sweetener, milk, cups, plates, eating utensils (there should be a drawer full of plastic forks), napkins, and anything else necessary for eating snacks. There will always be fresh milk and fruit available. Put this on the beverage table too.
   • Set the thermostats on "ON" so the fan runs continuously during the night. This does not mean the heat will be continuously on, just the fan to keep air circulating.

- Close all classroom doors down the hallway and to the auditorium.

4. When guests arrive, greet them warmly and make a general announcement that includes the location of the bathroom (the one behind the baptistry for men and the downstairs women's restroom for women), departure time (6:30 A.M.) as well as the fact that there is no smoking in the building, only outside by the kitchen door. If we have only male guests, use the downstairs ladies' restroom for them since it has more than one commode.

5. If there are not enough blankets sent, we own a few. HOWEVER, MAKE VERY SURE OUR BLANKETS ARE NOT SENT BACK THE NEXT MORNING.

6. Put out the toiletries box. These items are free for the taking.

7. We have some clothing in the puppet room which guests are welcome to; however, someone must stay in the room while they are making their selections. Lock the door when not in use.

8. Lights out is 10:00 P.M. or earlier if quite a few people have already gone to bed. Guests don't have to go to bed then. Keep lights on in the kitchen for anyone who wants to stay up awhile, then turn them out.

9. *Make sure the kitchen is clean* before _____ comes in to fix breakfast at 5:30. Keep the back door unlocked.

10. Complete the Room in the Inn volunteer record that is sent with the evening driver. Be sure to include all hours and mileage—estimate time and mileage from the food people, drivers, and others, and include mileage for the van for two round trips downtown. These records are an important part of our matching funds records.

11. Wake-up is 5:45 A.M.
    - Get blankets and towels from each guest—we must return as many as are sent the night before. *We return blankets and towels—do not return OUR blankets and sheets.*
    - Direct the guests to take the sheets off their mattresses, wipe the mattresses and stack them in the puppet room. There are sponges and spray cans in the puppet room window for this purpose.
    - Put all our dirty sheets—and any blankets that are used—in a garbage bag (which are in the puppet room) and leave the

bag in the puppet room. Someone will pick them up for laundering later. DO NOT SEND OUR SHEETS OR ANY OF OUR BLANKETS AND TOWELS BACK IN THE MORNING. They will be lost in the Room in the Inn laundering process forever!

12. Mop the areas we use. Equipment and cleaning supplies, with instructions, are in the puppet room.

13. Reset thermostats to automatic. Make sure the building is locked when you leave. Return the keys to the monthly captain or to (coordinator) by Sunday. *DO NOT leave them in the building.*

14. The morning driver should return the van to the area under the street light in front of the building and make sure the lights are off and the van is locked. *Do not leave the keys in the church building.* Return them to the monthly captain or (coordinator) prior to the next week.

THANKS FOR YOUR WILLINGNESS TO HOST OUR GUESTS! EVEN THOUGH THIS SEEMS TO BE A LONG LIST OF THINGS TO DO, REMEMBER THAT OUR PRIMARY ROLE IS AS HOSTS AND HOSTESSES IN GOD'S NAME WHO ARE EAGER TO HELP, LISTEN, TALK AND MAKE OUR GUESTS FEEL THAT THEY ARE CARED FOR. HAVE A GOOD EVENING!

SAMPLE C:
MISCELLANEOUS TIPS AND POINTERS

1. Welcome the guests and outline all rules immediately, including items like lights out, smoking, off-limits, wake-up call, etc. Explain the ticket system, its procedure and purpose.

2. Many congregations provide things like socks, underwear, hats, gloves, small containers of deodorant, toothpaste, soap, shampoo, etc. A great way for younger members of the congregation to get involved.

3. Decaffeinated products are better at night.

4. Some items are difficult to eat, e.g., apples, raw carrots, hard candy.
5. Guests enjoy generous portions of all kinds of food. Finger food and snacks alone are not enough to satisfy them after a long day.
6. Check the heating system. Some systems are on a timer and operate at a lower temperature during the night, resulting in some uncomfortable hours.
7. Report any major problems or concerns to the downtown center at (phone).
8. It is suggested that at least two volunteers be on duty, even overnight (one male always).
9. Have an emergency kit handy. Consult a doctor/nurse for contents.
10. Have a fire extinguisher in an accessible place.
11. Completely fill out form sent out each evening, give back to driver, and ask that he or she personally return it to downtown center staff. This form helps us in evaluating the ongoing program, identifies problems, and details services provided.
12. Post EMERGENCY NUMBERS (not found on printed brochure)
    Room in the Inn Center _____
    Congregation Coordinator _____
    Driver _____
    Medical person _____
    Someone who can respond to maintenance problem

    _____

E.S.P. (EMERGENCY SNOW PLAN)
In case of snow, there will be several downtown sites to accommodate those congregations unable to get downtown. Each congregation that evening needs to be on stand-by for any last-minute changes.

SAMPLE D:
Room in the Inn
Status Sheet

Emergency Numbers
Police/Ambulance   **911**
Metropolitan General Hospital   **(phone)**

Date _____

Guest Arrival Time _____

Guest Departure Time _____

Number of Guests: Male _____

                         Female _____

                         Children _____

                         Total _____

Volunteers Involved

_____   _____

_____   _____

_____   _____

_____   _____

_____   _____

Problems Encountered/Action Taken

_____

_____

_____

_____

_____

Special Comments

_____

_____

_____

_____

Items Needed

_____   _____   _____

_____   _____   _____

_____   _____   _____